If I Could Pray Again

Copyright © 2019. All rights reserved.

No part of this publication may be reproduced, stored in a retrieval system or transmitted in any way by any means, electronic, mechanical, photocopy, recording or otherwise, without the prior permission of the author except as provided by USA copyright law.

The opinions expressed by the author are not necessarily those of Publisher.

Book design Copyright © 2019. All rights reserved.

Library of Congress Control Number: 2019935884

RWG Publishing

PO Box 596 Litchfield, IL 62056

https://rwgpublishing.com/

If I Could Pray Again

When Nothing Less Than a Miracle Will Do

Trecia Willcutt

The proceeds from this book will go to Solomon's Porch.

A church that financially supports healing

and miracle services and Christian

education.

Table of Contents

Acknowledgements xi
Introduction xiii
Day 1...The Day the News Came 1
Day 2...The Day Our Miracle-In-The-Making Came 5
Day 3...The Day the Heartbreak Came 9
Day 4...The Day the Flood Came 13
Day 5...The Day the Disappointment Came 17
Day 6...The Day the Fear Came 21
Day 7...The Day the Sadness Came 25
Day 8...The Day the Depression Came 29
Day 9...The Day the First Change Came 33
Day 10...The Day the Anger Came 37
Day 11...The Day the Homecoming Came 41
Day 12...The Day the Discouragement Came 44
Day 13...The Day the Pain Came 47
Day 14...The Day the Death Came 51
Day 15...The Day the Rage Came 55
Day 16...The Day the Second Change Came 59
Day 17...The Day the Isolation Came 63
Day 18...The Day the Discord and Strife Came 67
Day 19...The Day the Self-Pity Came 71

Day 20...The Day the Separation Came 75

Day 21...The Day the Desperation Came 79

Day 22...The Day the Reality Came 83

Day 23...The Day the Decision Came 87

Day 24...The Day the Holy Spirit Came 91

Day 25...The Day the Love Came............................. 93

Day 26...The Day the Weeping Came 97

Day 27...The Day the Forgiveness Came 103

Day 28...The Day the Faith Came........................... 107

Day 29...The Day the Restoration Came 111

Day 30...The Day the Miracle Came 113

Day 31...The Day the Salvation Came 115

Evrett's Story 117

Author's Note 121

If I Could Pray that Prayer Again Words & Music by: Stacey Willcutt 123

*To my grandson, Evrett, who has
brought to my life faith, hope,
and love in a way I never
imagined possible!*

To the reader: It is my hope that the prayers in this book will bring to you and your family the same peace, comfort, encouragement, and results they brought to my family and me!

Acknowledgments

First, I would like to thank my husband, Stacey, who has traveled every step of this journey with me. Thank you for waking up at 3:00 am for many weeks and praying endlessly with me for our miracle-in-the making. Thank you for your steadfast faith in Evrett's healing. Thank you for pursuing after the promises of God with a fervency and never giving up on our grandson! Thank you for only speaking faith during those times when my heart was weeping. Thank you for traveling this journey with me in joy, in love, in peace, and in victory! I am blessed, and I am thankful to have you by my side. Thank you.

Next, I would like to thank my children, all of them. A journey like this is not traveled alone. It involves the entire family, and it affects the entire family. Thank you, Sam and Kascey, for the beautiful gift of Evrett. Thank you for allowing us to be part of this journey with you and entrusting your children into our care. Thank you, Jeff and Katelynn, for your support of everyone throughout this journey. Thank you for opening your home and your family to your nieces. Thank you for giving your love and your time to help whenever there was a need. Thank you, Jadon, for sharing your senior year of high school with your nieces and nephew without complaining, ever. All of you children make me proud. What a blessing to see the family come together, love each other, and help each other so selflessly.

Finally, I would like to thank our extended family, church family, and friends. Thank you for your continual prayers. Thank you for your compassion for my family. Thank you for pouring your love and financial support out upon my children. Thank you for weeping with us, and thank you for celebrating with us. My family is extremely blessed to have all of you follow us on this journey. I can only imagine the amount of prayers that you have all prayed on our behalf. Thank you for loving my family and helping us through this journey. All of you are so very much appreciated!

Introduction

This is a story about a journey. This journey is not like the other journeys in my life that I choose to go on by the decisions I conscientiously made. This journey is different. This journey was not chosen by the people who went on it. This journey is not the kind of journey that a person would ever willingly choose to take. In the beginning, I never would have chosen this journey, but now I cannot imagine my life without having traveled it. This journey has taught me things I might have missed altogether, such as; experiencing a depth of love I had never known before, discovering a way to find hope in the most desperate, darkest hours of need, obtaining an unshakeable faith, and securing a place of peace that this world has no access to! Now, I am most thankful for this journey. I feel extremely, abundantly, blessed to have been chosen to take this journey.

This journey began when my son and daughter-in-love received a doctor's report confirming that something was wrong with their unborn son. A virus had crossed the blood barrier and attacked my grandson's brain development, causing severe health impairments. We soon found out that our precious baby boy was going to need much more than just a healing; he was going to need a miracle! So the journey began. A journey in the pursuit of the supernatural. A journey in the pursuit of the miraculous. A journey in the pursuit of Jesus, for that is where supernatural miracles come from!

Before we get into the details of the journey, I would like to share some biblical truths concerning healings and miracles. This is by no means an exhaustive teaching on healings and miracles. To cover the entire subject effectively would require an entire book of its own. However, there are a few biblical truths that I believe are significant factors in understanding how a person receives a healing or a miracle. First, in order to receive healings and miracles I believe it is extremely imperative to understand where sickness and disease come from. Unfortunately, many people believe that God 'makes' people sick in order to gain some kind of glory out of it. Others believe that God 'lets' people get a sickness or disease in order to teach them a lesson. These beliefs are both contrary to the word of God because sickness and diseases do not come from God; sickness and diseases come from sin, the fall of man, and the curse of the law.

> Genesis 2:16-17—And the Lord God commanded the man, saying, of every tree of the garden thou may freely eat: But of the tree of the knowledge of good and evil, thou shalt not eat of it: for in the day that thou eat thereof thou shall die.

> Deuteronomy 28:15, 21-61—But it shall come to pass, if thou wilt not hearken unto the voice of the Lord thy God, to observe to do all his commandments and his statutes which I command thee this day; that all these curses shall come upon thee, and overtake thee, (21-61 briefly

paraphrased) panic, anxiety, plagues, pestilence, lung disease , fever, inflammation, arthritis, infections, illnesses, and injuries, boils, tumors, insanity, dementia, depression, schizophrenia, hysteria, blindness, bewilderment in your mind and memory, weak knees, weak legs, skin diseases, and every plague and every sickness that is not written in the book of this law will come upon you.

Healings and miracles come from God; from the redemptive works of Jesus which were finalized on the Cross of Calvary! Jesus redeemed us from the curse of the law and the fall of man, where sickness and diseases originated.

Galatians 3:13—Christ redeemed us from the curse of the law by becoming a curse for us, for it is written: Cursed is everyone that hangeth on a tree.

Isaiah 53:5—but he was wounded for our transgressions, he was bruised for our iniquities: the chastisement of our peace was upon him; and with his stripes we are healed.

1 Peter 2:24—who his own self bare our sins in his own body on the tree, that we, being dead to sins, should live unto righteousness: by whose stripes ye were healed.

The next biblical truth that is significant in receiving healings and miracles is to know who God is. God is the creator, not the destroyer: Genesis 1: 27: So God created man in his own image, in the image of God created he him; male and female created he them. Was God sick? Did God have cancer? Did God have heart disease? High blood pressure? Arthritis? Was God blind? Deaf? Did God have a mental illness? No, and we were not created to be that way either. God did not create mankind only to destroy us by sickness and disease. I can most closely relate to this when I think about my children. I did not give birth to my children only to destroy them in some way. I would not 'make' one of my children drink poison and then take care of him in order to gain the praise of other people. I would not 'let' one of my children run with a sharp knife to teach him the lesson that running with a sharp knife is dangerous. God, in no wise, treats his children this way either. No, our heavenly Father made provisions to deliver us from sickness and diseases through the gifts of healings and the working of miracles.

In 1 John 1:5, John does a beautiful job describing who God is: God is light, and in him is no darkness at all. Then, in James 1:17 we learn that: Every good gift and every perfect gift is from above and cometh down from the Father of lights, with whom is no variableness, neither shadow of turning. God sent his son, Jesus Christ, to heal every manner of sickness and disease. Acts 10:38 records: God anointed Jesus of Nazareth with the Holy Spirit and power, who went about doing good and healing all who were oppressed of the devil; for God was with him. This scripture confirms where sickness and disease comes from: the devil, the enemy of your soul!

Many people are deceived by the enemy into thinking that God 'let' sickness and disease attack their children, their loved ones, and even their self. The danger in that deceitful lie is that then people begin being angry with God and asking, "God, why are you letting this happen?

You're God, why won't you do something?" I believe it is a difficult task to receive healings and miracles from someone you are angry with, someone you might even hate, someone you believe is responsible for your pain, heartbreak, and brokenness. That is why it is so important to know who God is. He is the creator of life, and God sent his Son, Jesus, so that we might have life and life more abundantly! (John 10:10). What is abundant about sickness and disease? God simply is not two different people: he does not plague people with sickness and diseases and then send his Son to heal people of the sicknesses and diseases that he put on them.

The final biblical truth that I will address in this book concerning receiving healings and miracles is the truth of who your enemy is. Your enemy is not God! God did not make your child sick. God did not make your loved one sick. God did not make you sick. God does not make people sick. The enemy does that. Jesus described our enemy this way, "The thief comes to steal, kill, and to destroy (John 10:10). Peter described our enemy this way, "your adversary the devil, as a roaring lion, walketh about, seeking whom he may devour (1 Peter 5:8). Moses described our enemy this way, "Now the serpent was more subtil than any beast of the field" (Genesis 3:1). The enemy comes to destroy our health, our children, our families, our lives, and then he subtly convinces us that it is God's fault so that we will turn away from the only hope we have of receiving our healing or our miracle! It is imperative that you know who your enemy is and how your enemy operates so you will not be led away from the truth. The truth that the enemy is the one who brings sickness and disease and God is the one who gives the gift of healings and miracles.

Jesus said this about the devil, "he was a murderer from the beginning, not holding to the truth, for there is no truth in him. When he lies, he speaks his native language, for he is a liar and the father of lies." (John 8:44 NIV). The devil will try many different lies to hold people captive to sickness and diseases. The devil will tell you that you are being punished. That it must not be God's will for you to be healed or you would be. That everyone has to die of something; it just must be God's plan. The devil will also continually blame God for the sickness or disease by posing subtle accusations such as; "why does God let that happen to innocent children? How can a loving God let your child suffer? God could do something if he wanted to!" You must know who God is and you must know who your enemy is so you will not be deceived by the devil's lies!

I am thankful that I learned these biblical truths before this journey began. Knowing these truths is what will bring the much-needed healings and miracles to my children, to my family, and to my grandson! I would not want to travel this wonderful journey without knowing the truth of God's word, God's plan, God's nature, God's Son, and God's promises! Now, on to the journey.

Day 1

The Day the News Came

*But whoso looketh into the perfect law of liberty,
and continueth therein, he being not a forgetful hearer,
but a doer of the work, this man shall be blessed in his
deed...James 1:25*

It was August 14, 2017, the first day of the new school year. It was a busy day as every first day of school is. I was in my office when I got the call. I was expecting the call from my daughter-in-love with an update on her six-month routine checkup. However, I was not expecting what she told me, "Something is wrong with the baby; they are sending me to the hospital." I quickly responded, "What? Why do they think something is wrong with the baby?" She proceeded to tell me that she had not been feeling him move as much lately, so she mentioned it to her doctor. Her doctor then decided to do an ultrasound to see if there might be something going on. There was. Her doctor wasted no time and immediately sent my daughter-in-love to the hospital for further tests.

Without even consciously thinking I stood up from my desk and started praying over the phone, "I bind the spirit of fear in the name of Jesus. Devil, you take your hands off my grandson right now. I pray for peace and comfort to come over my daughter." I then told my principal I had to leave, and I drove home. By this time, my son had left work and met my husband and me at our house, and we all drove the 45 minutes to the hospital together. During the drive, we were all in agreement that no matter what evil report was trying to invade our lives, we would believe the report of the Lord. We would believe for divine healing for whatever it was that my unborn grandson needed healing for.

My daughter-in-love was dismissed from the hospital that evening after being scheduled for a series of additional tests the following week at a different hospital which was more equipped to run advanced ultrasounds and MRI's. Outside of the hospital we all stood together on the sidewalk and declared a prayer of agreement. We all held hands and agreed that we would not accept anything other than health, wholeness, and healing for this unborn child that we all loved so much already.

I believed in our prayer of agreement, and I believe my children did also. But I did not know what was ahead of us, nor did they. I did not understand or even imagine what this journey would entail. I thought this trial was about praying for the faith it would take to receive a miracle.

But if I could pray again...

Oh, Heavenly Father, I ask that you set my children's hearts on Romans 12:12 and give them the revelation of rejoicing in hope, being patient in tribulation, and continuing instant in prayer. Reveal to their hearts and minds the promise of Romans 5:2-4: that by faith, they can have peace with you through this situation. Help my children rejoice in their hope which is in Jesus and through his grace, so they can glory in this tribulation, which will work patience, patience will work experience, experience will work hope, and by their hope, the love of God will be shed aboard in their hearts by the Holy Ghost. Lord, I ask that you fill them with all joy and peace in believing, that they may never lose their hope through the power of the Holy Spirit (Romans 15:13). I speak Hebrews 10:36 into their spirits right now, that they may feast everyday on knowing that they have need of patience continually and that after they have done the will of God by standing by faith, they will receive the promise. As quickly as my children entered this trial; they will want this trial to end. Help them, Lord, to comprehend James 1:2-3 and be able to truly count it all joy for falling into this trial; knowing that the trying of their faith will work the patience they will need for the road ahead. That when patience has her perfect work, my children will be made perfect and entire, wanting nothing because they will have, by being patient, received the promise! Finally, Father, I ask in the name of Jesus, that you strengthen my children with all might, according to your glorious power, unto all patience and longsuffering with joyfulness so that they are able to endure this journey with gladness (Colossians 1:11). Amen.

Day 2

The Day Our Miracle-In-The Making Came

(God) Who does great things, unfathomable and wondrous works without number...Job 9:10 (NASB)

Oh, how I remember that day. It was around lunchtime when my daughter-in-love called to tell me she was at her doctor's appointment and the baby was unresponsive. She was being sent to the hospital again, and she wondered if I could come and get my granddaughter because she was unable to get ahold of my son while he was at work. When I got to the hospital the doctors were monitoring the baby, and he seemed to be responding with a strong heartbeat and some movement. What a relief we felt at that moment. However, the doctors were undecided on the next course of action.

Within an hour the decision had been made; the doctors were going to deliver my grandson as soon as my son could get to the hospital. We were having a baby today. At 32 weeks, we were having a baby. At a projected birthweight of 2 lbs. 9 oz., we were having a baby. Angel One from Children's Hospital had been called in to transport my grandson to the NICU right after he was born. As my daughter-in-love was being prepared for an emergency cesarean birth, I will never forget the look on my son's face as he went back to gown-up himself. Oh, how he wanted to be happy, elated, and excited about the birth of his first son, but the sheer worry of what we had been told to prepare for had overridden all other emotions.

We watched the medics from Angel One come through the elevator doors and enter the nursery. The nursery blinds were still open, so we were able to watch them set up the incubator and everything else needed for a premature, high-risk birth. However, within just a few minutes the nursery blinds were closed, and we knew that our precious baby boy had made his arrival. While trying to peak through every crack in the blinds possible, we finally found one crack that we were able to see through which just so happened to be directly in front of the incubator. I stood there and watched through a one-inch crack in the blinds a nurse bring my grandson into the nursery and place him in a plastic bed.

A medic immediately placed a bag on my grandson's mouth and started artificial respiration. A doctor was frantically moving around doing I don't know what along with about four other nurses, technicians, and medics. Medical bags with instruments were being opened, tubes were being unrolled, needles were being unwrapped, and the entire time one medic was steadily breathing air into my grandson through that bag. I do not know how much time passed, but all of sudden everyone's rushed movement slowed down until it stopped completely. The doctor turned around and pulled his gown and gloves off, threw them in the trash, and walked away. The medic pulled the bag off my grandson's mouth and placed it on a cart beside him. I held my breath and refused to think about what might have just happened.

I did not say anything to my husband who was sitting nearby reading his Bible. I did not say anything to my daughter-in-love's mom who was standing off to the side. I just stood there and watched, waiting for something to happen. A nurse walked over to the plastic bed and wrapped my grandson in a blanket. I thought my grandson was gone. I thought they were preparing to take him to his mom and dad so they could say good-bye to their precious baby boy. I just stood there; still, quiet, and watching, refusing to accept that this is how our miracle would end. I put my head down and said to myself, "NO, this cannot be happening!" In a few minutes, the nurse then unwrapped my grandson from the blanket, picked him up, and turned around toward the one-inch crack I was looking through. She lifted him up over the sides of the plastic bed, and when she did, I saw little arms and legs moving! I cried out, "He's alive!" and then I dropped my head again and said, "Thank you, Jesus!"

But if I could pray again...

Dear Heavenly Father, I come to you in the name of your dear Son, Jesus Christ, and I ask that you put a song in my children's hearts to talk of all your wondrous works and to remember them continually (1 Chronicles 16:9,12). Let my children lift up their voices over the next part of this journey and declare: blessed be the Lord God of Israel who only doeth wondrous things (Psalm 72:18). Fix their hearts and minds on Psalm 86:10; for you are great Lord and doest wondrous things, you art God alone. I pray that every time the enemy comes and tries to plant a seed of fear, doubt, or unbelief that Psalm 107:8 rises up in my children and they shout in spiritual defense; we give thanks unto Jehovah for his loving-kindness and for his wondrous works. We praise the one who alone does great and wondrous things, for his gracious love is everlasting (Psalm 136:4). Cover my children in a spirit of praise and let them only speak of your glorious honor and your majesty and your wondrous works (Psalm 145:5) in Jesus name. Amen.

Day 3

The Day the Heartbreak Came

*He heals the brokenhearted and
binds up their wounds...Psalm 147:3 (ESV)*

I went back to work the week after my grandson was born. However, the first day back I quickly realized that I wanted and needed to be with my family. I arranged to work half days for a week, and then I would decide where to go from there. My family was my first priority. On my third half-day back I left work, and went to pick up my oldest granddaughter from school. I was going to take her to the hospital that day to see her baby brother. My daughter-in-love called me to tell me the results of the MRI my grandson had the previous day. She began reciting all that the doctors had told her. The only two words I can remember her saying were ventilator and stroke. Our precious Evrett had a stroke before he was even born. Then these words followed, "And your son did not take the news very well." I felt like I had the breath physically knocked out of me. I began crying so uncontrollably I had to pull over on the side of the road. I could no longer even talk to my daughter-in-love, and I told her that I would have to call her back.

My heart broke in a way that day that I had never experienced before in my entire life. The thought that my son had to listen to what the doctors were telling him about his son was just more than I could wrap my mind or my heart around. What I did not know then is that many more doctor's reports would follow in the coming weeks and months. I would have to stand back and watch my children hear repeatedly, day after day, week after week, and month after month, endless, hopeless, and life-robbing diagnoses and prognoses. Every time it knocked the breath out of me again just like it did on that first day. The heartbreak had only begun.

As soon as I got to the hospital, I began reassuring my son that everything would be all right. With everything in me, I wanted to make it all go away for my children. Somehow, I wanted my words of encouragement to erase the heartbreak that had been inflicted on my children by the words of the doctor's reports. With a smile on my face I boldly declared, "We're believing for a miracle, the Lord will see us through this!" All of that is still true.

But if I could pray again...

Oh, Heavenly Father how I cry out to you right now for my children. Lord you know the pain their hearts have endured today. Your word declares that you are close to the brokenhearted and save those who are crushed in spirit (Psalm 34:18). Let my children feel the closeness of your Holy Spirit right now. Lord, my children have heard many evil reports today. They have been told that their son has many impairments and obstacles to overcome. Reveal the powerful promise of Psalm 34:19 to their hearts and minds today that although many are the afflictions of the righteous: you, Lord, delivereth him out of them all. Speak to their spirits that this situation is not without hope, it is not beyond repair, and it is not beyond your promises! Holy Spirit, comfort my children according to Psalm 39:12 which promises them that you will hear their prayer, O Lord, and give ear to their cry; and you will not withhold your peace at their tears! With every tear my children shed, I declare the peace of God covers their hearts and minds in the name of Jesus! Amen.

Day 4

The Day the Flood Came

*We are troubled on every side, yet not distressed;
we are perplexed, but not in despair, persecuted but not forsaken;
cast down, but not destroyed...2 Corinthians 4:8-9*

After numerous tests, my children were told that my daughter-in-love had contracted a virus that crossed the blood barrier. The virus attacked my grandson, and we were told that it had affected the development of his brain; actually, we were told that the third section of his brain was missing altogether. This section of the brain is responsible for seeing, hearing, sucking and swallowing, along with many other motor skills; like breathing. We were numb really. It just did not seem real. One month ago, we had a healthy baby boy on the way, and now we were told that everything had drastically changed in just a few short weeks.

My children were bombarded with even more doctor's reports and upcoming procedures, which consisted of hydrocephalus, blindness, and deafness, genetic testing which included Down syndrome, chronic lung disease, heart complications, shunt surgery, a feeding tube, and a breathing tube. As if that news was not enough, then there were concerns about his ability to regulate his own body temperature and every other possible complication that is included in a premature birth.

I can remember feeling so overwhelmed. We were told that there were so many different things wrong with our precious Evrett that I did not even know what ailment, complication, or procedure to start praying for first. With every additional report, I would continue to speak words of encouragement to my children. I always had a scripture to share with them to add to their prayer journal, "there's nothing too hard for the Lord, it doesn't matter what is wrong the Lord heals ALL thy diseases!"

But if I could pray again...

Our most gracious Heavenly Father, I ask that you bring to life Isaiah 43:1-2 in my children's hearts right now, "Fear not, for I have redeemed you; I have called you by name, you are mine. When you pass through the waters, I will be with you; and through the rivers, they shall not overwhelm you; when you walk through fire you shall not be burned, and the flame shall not consume you." Grant to my children a divine understanding that you are with them and you will carry them through this fiery trial! Let them take refuge and comfort in knowing that although the waters are raging and the fire is burning, they are divinely protected by your Holy Spirit. I pray my children will continue to call upon you in the day of trouble because you have promised to deliver them (Psalm 50:15). You, Lord, are their stronghold in this time of trouble (Nahum 1:7) and I pray they never turn their hearts away from your word. Father, in the name of Jesus, I also ask that you make known to them this hour that you are their refuge and strength in this situation. You are a very present help in trouble, and you hear the cries of your children (Psalm 46:1). Thank you, Lord, for helping my children through this. Thank you for keeping them protected by your mercy and grace. Thank you, Lord, that I can take comfort knowing that this fire will not consume my children! Amen.

Day 5

The Day the Disappointment Came

*The heart of man plans his way,
but the Lord establishes his steps...Proverbs 16:9 (ESV)*

For the first six weeks of Evrett's life we were all extremely joyful that he had survived, was able to breathe on his own without a ventilator, and was gaining weight. However, his weight gain also brought about another decision; once Evrett weighed five lbs., the doctors wanted to implant a shunt to drain the water off his brain. We did not want this surgery. We wanted healing, we wanted our miracle, and we wanted to take our precious baby boy home!

Not only were my children told that they would have to put Evrett on a ventilator in order to perform the surgery, but they were also informed about every other possible complication of using anesthesia on a newborn. Looking back though, I think the most dreaded news was that the surgery would delay Evrett coming home for an additional six weeks. At that time, we could not fathom another six weeks in NICU. Another six weeks of the family living apart; my daughter-in-love at the hospital, the granddaughters with me during the day and at home with my son at night. Another six weeks of weekend trips to the hospital so the children could see their mom. It was just inconceivable.

My daughter-in-love called me and wanted us to have our entire church stand with her and my son in agreement that Evrett would not need this surgery; that the fluid from his brain would begin to drain on its own. We did. Evrett was still scheduled for surgery, and we were still praying he would not need it. The morning of the surgery, my daughter-in-love called to tell me the surgery had been canceled. I was so relieved; it had to be a sign that we were going to see our miracle manifest! However, within a few short days the surgery had been rescheduled. In spite of our disappointment we continued praying every day, and hoping for another cancellation. What we got instead was an unexpected call from a nurse the day before the scheduled surgery informing my daughter-in-love that the surgery had been moved up; Evrett would be going to surgery in less than two hours.

I was shocked really. We had watched the Lord work so many wonderful things in little Evrett over the last few weeks; he could see, he could hear, he was sucking a pacifier. These were all things we were told would never be possible—if he even survived. We believed he would never need a shunt. Now, we were being told it was going to happen anyway. The shock soon turned in to a gauntlet of emotions: nervousness, fear, worry, anxiety, and confusion, but looking back, mostly disappointment.

Disappointment that our prayers were not answered the way we had hoped. Disappointment that Evrett was not healed yet. Disappointment because things were not working out as we wanted them to. Disappointment that the hospital stay would be longer than what we expected.

Although my daughter-in-love was staying close by the hospital, my son was at home when he received the news that the surgery had been moved up. The hospital was over an hour away. My prayer was, "Dear Lord, let my son make it the hospital safely before the surgery so he can spend time with Evrett before they take him back."

But if I could pray again...

Dear Heavenly Father, I come to you in the name of your dear Son, Jesus Christ, and I ask that you help my children understand and trust in Isaiah 55:8-9: For my thoughts are not your thoughts, neither are your ways my ways, saith the Lord. For as the heavens are higher than the earth, so are my ways higher than your ways, and my thoughts higher than your thoughts. The news they have just received goes against everything their hearts desired and their prayers have asked for, so Lord, I'm asking you to help my children to trust in you with all their heart; and lean not unto their own understanding. In the midst of this situation, lead them to acknowledge you in all their ways so you can direct their path forward (Proverbs 3:5-6). As it is promised in 2 Timothy 2:7, give them understanding in all things today. Let this divine understanding supersede the disappointment they are being attacked by right now. Finally, I ask you Lord to help my children take comfort in Romans 8:28 knowing that all things work together for good to them that love God, to them who are the called according to his purpose. I pray your word will override the disappointment and that my children will focus on your promises and know that you are working out something very good. Amen.

Day 6

The Day the Fear Came

*He is not afraid of bad news; his heart is firm,
trusting in the Lord. His heart is steady; he will not be afraid,
until he looks in triumph on his adversaries...Psalm 112:7-8 (ESV)*

Two days after the shunt surgery, the doctors tried to remove the ventilator. Evrett was unable to breathe on his own, and the doctors immediately intubated him again. The doctors reassured us they would try again in a couple of days when he was stronger. They did and that time it was successful. We were extremely relieved and very thankful. However, the surgery seemed to set Evrett back in almost every way. It was almost like starting all over again but now adding one more obstacle. Evrett was struggling to breathe on his own after being on the vent. This created a domino effect with regulating his own body temperature and blood pressure, in addition to being in constant pain and discomfort. The doctors kept telling us that it would take him time to recover from the surgery and get back to where he was. Then, after a week or so, we began to see some improvement.

I was sitting at the kitchen table when I received the call from my daughter-in-love. She was crying as she sobbed, "Evrett coded." I responded abruptly, "Evrett coded? What? He's been making such good progress, what happened?" My daughter-in-love began telling me what had happened. She was holding Evrett, and he just stopped breathing. The nurse put him back in his incubator and began doing chest compressions. Evrett was unresponsive, so the nurse called for additional medical help. They continued CPR; my daughter-in-love could not stand to watch because she was afraid Evrett would continue to be unresponsive. She did not think she could stand there and watch her baby die. She walked down the hallway to call and let me know what was going on.

I cannot tell you how helpless I felt at that moment. My grandson was in cardiopulmonary arrest and unable to breathe on his own, and my daughter-in-love was there by herself; without anyone to tell her it was all going to be Ok. Without anyone to comfort her, console her, or cry with her, and without anyone to sit with her while she waited to hear whatever news the doctor's would bring. I stayed on the phone with her and began to pray, "Lord, I rebuke this fear from attacking my daughter-in-love. I pray you give her peace and comfort right now, knowing that we are going to receive the miracle you promised us."

But if I could pray again...

Father in the name of Jesus, I ask that you send your Holy Spirit to comfort my daughter-in-love this very second and let her know that she does not have anything to fear because you are with her. She does not have to be dismayed; for you are her God: and you will strengthen her in this very moment; you will help her, and you will uphold her with the right hand of your righteousness (Isaiah 41:10). Lord, your word says that you have not given us a spirit of fear but of power, love, and a sound mind (2 Timothy 1:7). I rebuke this spirit of fear that is attacking my daughter-in-love, and I command it to be cast down in the name of Jesus. Bless my daughter-in-love right now with a spirit of power, love, and a sound mind. Lord, as my daughter-in-love seeks you in this situation, your word promises that you will hear her and deliver her from all her fears (Psalm 34:4). Finally, Father reveal to her heart the promise of Joshua 1:9: Be strong and of a good courage; be not afraid, neither be thou dismayed: for the Lord thy God is with thee whithersoever thou goest. Thank you, Lord, that even though we are not with her at this very moment, you are! Comfort her, love her, wrap her in your arms, and let her know that you are with her wherever this journey takes her! Amen.

Day 7

The Day the Sadness Came

*Cast your burden on the Lord, and he will sustain you;
he will never permit the righteous to be moved...Psalm 55:22 (ESV)*

The first few weeks after my grandson was born turned into a blur. We, as a family, were trying to get arrangements made for some type of daily routine. My daughter-in-love had applied to stay at the Ronald McDonald house. My son was trying to determine how much time he could take off work, and I had applied for an extended leave from my work to take care of Evrett's sisters; one in second grade and one not even two years old. After two weeks, my son returned to work. I kept the granddaughters during the day, and he picked them up when he got off work. My daughter-in-love stayed at the hospital, and my son took the girls down on Friday and returned home with them on Sunday.

It was physically and emotionally exhausting on everyone, but my children still held on to the promise of our miracle. Everyone pulled together, and we just did what we had to do. My children were hopeful and positive and talked about all that the Lord had done and was continuing to do in Evrett's little body. However, days turned into weeks; weeks full of one bad report after another, weeks full of new concerns and obstacles, weeks full of undue amounts of stress, and weeks full of the family being separated.

I remember the first time my daughter-in-love came home from the hospital for the weekend. I pulled up in the driveway to drop something off, and her, my son, and my granddaughters were all in the front yard. There was a look of such relief on all their faces. My daughter-in-love was relieved to be home, my son was relieved not to be spending the weekend at the hospital, and my granddaughters were relieved to be at home with both of their parents.

As much relief as that day brought to all of them; it would soon change. It was not long until the next look I saw on my children's faces was a look of sadness. Sadness that the whole family was not at home together. Sadness that when my daughter-in-love was at home, she was not with her newborn son. Sadness that the family was still separated because Evrett was not well enough to come home. Sadness that the days had turned to weeks. Sadness that our miracle still had not manifested. Sadness that more reports, more obstacles, and more time was passing without Evrett being completely healed.

Right before my eyes, I watched my children enter a great spiritual attack. Their joy had turned to sadness. Their hope had turned to fear, and the very foundation of their faith was being tried by fire. I knew it was happening. I literally saw it happening, and I tried so hard to encourage them with empty words like, "don't give up, our miracle is still on the way." I wanted my children to hold on and keep their faith strong. I even prayed, "Lord help them, they are growing weak, and they need you so much right now!"

But if I could pray again...

Father, in the name of Jesus, I ask that you minister to the broken hearts and sadness of my children. Holy Spirit move on them and make Isaiah 40:28-31 come alive in their spirits right now! Reveal the depth of this promise that the Lord is the everlasting God, the Creator of the ends of the earth. He will not grow tired or weary, and his understanding no one can fathom. Show my children that you give strength to the weary and you increase the power of the weak. Even youths grow tired and weary, and young men stumble and fall, but those who hope in the Lord will renew their strength. Reveal to my children that as they hope in you, they will soar on wings like eagles; they will run and not grow weary, they will walk and not be faint. Help my children to hope in you alone and renew their strength! Lord, I also pray that you move on my children's hearts not to give up on receiving your promise. Speak to their hearts to wait for you Lord; to be strong and take heart and wait for you Lord to manifest your promises (Psalm 27:14). Thank you, Lord. Amen.

Day 8

The Day the Depression Came

Casting all your care upon him, for he cares for you...1 Peter 5:7

It had been 74 days since our miracle-in-the-making arrived, and we were celebrating Thanksgiving without him. Evrett was still in NICU. Oh, how my daughter-in-love tried with everything in her to celebrate with the family. She tried so hard to smile, to visit, to enjoy her time with the family, but on the inside her heart was crying, "I want my son to be here with us!" It was a hard day for my daughter-in-love and looking back; something seemed to change around that time. I believe that was the day depression first made its appearance.

It was subtle at first, just a quiet sadness in her. She is such a quiet person anyway; I tried to pass it off as sheer exhaustion and being extremely overwhelmed. However, I know now that was not the case. My daughter-in-love was carrying a great burden. She was being forced to choose between her children: should she stay at the hospital with Evrett or come home and take care of her daughters? What mother can choose one child over another? What her heart wanted, she could not have. Whatever decision she made left her heart half-empty.

I tried to reassure her that she was a great mom, and that it was Ok for her to come home for a while and spend time with the girls. I reasoned with her that Evrett had full-time nursing care, and that he was being well taken care of. I did not want my daughter-in-love to feel guilty for not being at the hospital, but the internal conflict her heart was battling was written all over her face as tears flowed from her eyes. I prayed for my daughter-in-love that day, "Lord help her to make the decisions she needs to make, and help her to be at peace with them."

But if I could pray again...

Father, in the name of Jesus, I ask that your Holy Spirit compel my daughter-in-love to run into your presence knowing that because she has labored and is heavy laden, you will give her rest (Matthew 11:28). Lord, I speak the promise in Psalm 143:7-8 over her, that you will hear her speedily, O Lord: her spirit is failing: hide not your face from her. Cause her to hear your lovingkindness in the morning; for in you she must trust: cause her to know the way wherein she should walk, for I lift up her soul unto thee. You, Lord, are a shield for her, her glory, and the lifter up of her head (Psalm 3:3). I know you, Lord, are a refuge for the oppressed, a refuge in times of trouble, my daughter-in-love is in trouble, and she needs you Lord (Psalm 9:9). I pray that you turn her mourning into dancing and gird her with gladness (Psalm 30:11). Lord, your word promises that you will keep him in perfect peace, whose mind is stayed on thee: because he trusteth in thee. I pray my daughter-in-love will fully trust in the Lord forever: for in the Lord Jehovah is where she will find everlasting strength (Isaiah 26:3). During this time of attack reveal to her the power of 2 Samuel 22:2-3: The Lord is my rock, and my fortress, and my deliverer; The God of my rock; in him will I trust: he is my shield, and the horn of my salvation, my high tower, and my refuge, my Savior; thou savest me from violence. Finally, Lord, help her to understand that you will order her steps and though she may fall, she shall not be utterly cast down, for you, Lord, will uphold her with your hand (Psalm 37:23-24). Lord, I thank you for my daughter-in-love. She is precious to me, and I ask that you cover her in your grace and mercy that endureth forever! (Psalm 136). Amen.

Day 9

The Day the First Change Came

For the righteous falls seven times and rises again...
Proverbs 24:16 (ESV)

It had been many weeks since the birth of my grandson. Many weeks of sad news. Many weeks of waking up every day having to relive every doctor's report, every diagnosis, and every seemingly insurmountable obstacle. Many weeks of the family being separated and the girls being without both of their parents. Many weeks of living every day in a fiery trial with the forces of hell waging a continual war on our precious baby boy's health. Many weeks that took a toll on my son.

My son was beginning to change. The joy I once saw on his face as he would talk about how the Lord had something special planned for Evrett's life, was gone. The positive attitude about how the family would pull together and make it through this situation with the Lord's help was gone. The good mood he was in every morning when I picked the girls up was gone. The happiness he felt every afternoon when he picked the girls up after work was gone. The relief he once felt when his wife came home from the hospital to spend the weekend with the family was gone. Everything my son once thought was good seemed to be gone, and now in the place of good, anger began to take over.

I watched my son begin to turn away from everything good. He turned away from our church. He turned away from his musical gift in worship. He turned away from his job. He turned away from his wife. He turned away from his children. He turned away from me, and he turned away from the rest of the family. I watched this happen to my son, and I prayed, "Lord, help him turn back to the good things, help him turn back to you!"

But if I could pray again...

Oh, Heavenly Father, I cry out to you right now for my son! Reveal to him through your Holy Spirit that he is being tempted by the enemy because God tempts no man with evil! (James 1:13). Reveal to my son that he will be blessed by enduring this temptation and not giving in to wiles of the devil: for when he is tried, he shall receive the crown of life, which you, Lord, hath promised to them that love you (James 1:12). Holy Spirit, encourage my son to watch and pray so he will not enter into further temptation because his flesh is weak right now; strengthen my son's spirit! (Mark 14:38). I see what the adversary is doing, and I stand in the gap for my son and make intercession for him because your word says that if a man be overtaken in a fault, ye which are spiritual, restore such an one in the spirit of meekness (Ephesians 6:1). I restore my son to you, Lord. In this dark hour, move on my son and give him the deep understanding that we are serving a merciful Savior who is not a high priest which cannot be touched with the feeling of our infirmities. Help my son to see the truth, the truth that you have not abandoned him. You are not punishing him. You care about what he is going through, and you know how his heart is breaking. Give my son the knowledge to understand that you are waiting for him to come boldly unto the throne of grace, that he may obtain mercy, and find grace to help him in his time of need (Hebrews 4:15-16). I ask for these things in the name of Jesus. Amen.

Day 10

The Day the Anger Came

*Do not be overcome by evil,
but overcome evil with good...Romans 12:21 (ESV)*

It had been three months and our precious baby boy was still not home. Evrett was struggling with not being able to drink enough formula from a bottle to sustain himself. The doctors had decided a feeding tube would be the quickest way to get him home. The doctors reassured us that the feeding tube was just temporary. When Evrett was able to eat enough on his own the doctors would remove the tube from his stomach. So another surgery was scheduled. Another surgery that we knew would delay Evrett's homecoming for at least six more weeks.

By this time, the pain and heartbreak my son was carrying for his son had turned into anger. My son had withdrawn from everyone and everything. He was battling an intense anger inside of him that he carried every day. He was angry about everything. He was angry about nothing. He was angry that his son was not home. He was angry that his wife was not home. He was angry that he was at home. He was angry at his job, so he quit.

He even seemed to be angry with me, and he wanted me to know that he was angry. I knew.

The day of the feeding tube surgery was no different. My son was angry. We all gathered around Evrett's bed to pray before the doctors took him back, and my son led us in prayer. He tried to reach out to the Lord for help during this time, but his anger had overridden his heart. When I heard the anger in my son's voice, it pierced me to the very core. I began to weep inside for the brokenness I saw in my son. I so wanted him to run into the arms of his Savior. A Savior who is so full of mercy, love, and compassion, but the anger in my son seemed to be driving him away from his Savior. Then, I began to weep for my daughter-in-love because I know that when anger runs rampant it falls on those who are closest to you. I saw how anger was trying to consume my son, and I prayed, "Oh Jesus, how my son needs your love and compassion right now. Help my son to understand that being angry is only going to open the door to destruction!"

But if I could pray again...

Dear Heavenly Father, I pray that you help my son to enter into a rest in the Lord. Help my son to wait patiently for the Lord to move by his grace and mercy in this situation. Holy Spirit help my son to cease from anger and forsake the wrath that the enemy is tempting him with (Psalm 37:7-8). Help my son to understand that this anger will work against the righteousness of God, and that is why the enemy wants him to be angry (James 1:20). I pray that you help my son understand that by allowing anger to rule him he is not ruling over his own spirit, and a man who does not rule over his own spirit is like a city broken down and without walls; defenseless against the enemy (Proverbs 25:28). Rather, show my son that a man who is slow to anger is better than the mighty, and a man who rules his own spirit is greater than a mighty warrior who can take a city! (Proverbs 16:32). I ask that you give my son strength so he can rise up in his spirit and be a mighty warrior over this battle! Reveal the wisdom of Ephesians 4:31 to my son, that he will be wise to get rid of all bitterness, rage, and anger, brawling and slander, along with every form of malice. Move in my son's heart to pray, lifting up holy hands, without wrath and doubting (1 Timothy 2:8), so he can sing praises and tell of all the wondrous works of the Lord (Psalm 105:2). I ask for these things in Jesus name. Amen.

Day 11

The Day the Homecoming Came

*Happy is he that hath the God of Jacob for his help,
whose hope is in the Lord his God...Psalm 146:5*

It was finally here! We had been waiting 115 days for this day. The day Evrett would come home from the hospital. It was a beautiful, glorious day! We were all so excited to be bringing our precious baby boy home, finally. The only thing that overshadowed our celebration was the brokenness that had already taken place in my son and daughter-in-love. My son's anger had driven a wedge between him and almost everyone. We all seemed to walk on pins and needles; never knowing what might be said to who. Nevertheless, my daughter-in-love was so relieved to be going home so she could have all of her children together. However, I could see the overwhelming impact of the last 115 days of hurt, fear, worry, and physical exhaustion still on her face.

We had quite a celebration planned. The house was decorated. We had a cake waiting. We were bringing our baby boy home in style! We caravanned home from the hospital and had family ready and waiting to see our miracle-in-the-making, some for the very first time. I took pictures of my daughter-in-love pulling the wagon with Evrett in it out of the hospital. I took pictures of my son carrying Evrett into the house. I took pictures of one of my granddaughters seeing her baby cousin for the first time. I took pictures of my other daughter-in-love holding her nephew for the first time. I took pictures of everything. I was so happy to see my son and daughter-in-love home with ALL their children. It was a good day.

When I left their house that evening I began to praise the Lord for bringing Evrett home. I was so thankful for all the Lord had done, and all that the Lord was doing in Evrett's body. I continued to praise the Lord and thank Him for the miracle that we knew would completely manifest! I was so thankful that Evrett was home, but what I did not know that night was that Evrett would only be home for a short time. I prayed for my children that night, "Lord, give them strength and unity in their home and in their hearts, so they can raise these children in a home full of love, and a home full of your Holy Spirit."

But if I could pray again…

Dear Heavenly Father, I pray right now that you give my son and daughter-in-love supernatural strength to hold fast to the profession of their faith without wavering, knowing that you are faithful in your promises (Hebrews 10:23). Help them continually profess Evrett's healing no matter what they see with their natural eyes. Help my children to stay focused on you Lord, for you are their hope (Psalm 71:5). Lord, you promised that your eye is upon them that fear you and hope in your mercy. Let your mercy be upon my children as they put their hope in you (Psalm 33:18, 22). I pray a hunger upon my children's hearts and souls to read, pray, and study your word like never before. I pray that they both turn to your word for guidance, wisdom, and peace because this is how they will attain patience and comfort, so they are able to stand-fast and hold on to their hope in you (Romans 15:4). Father, I also ask that you reveal to them the importance of holding onto their hope in this situation. Help them understand in their hearts that hope that is seen is not hope: for if a person sees something they do not hope for it, but if they do not see it, then their hope will help them wait with patience until they do see it. Help my children understand that even though they do not see the manifestations of complete healing, that by continually hoping for it they will receive the promise of the Lord! For why would we be instructed to wait for something that was never going to happen? (Romans 8:24-25). Let my children declare that blessed is the man that trusts in the Lord, and whose hope the Lord is! (Jeremiah 17:7). I ask for all of these things in Jesus name. Amen.

Day 12

The Day the Discouragement Came

*Be of good courage, and he shall strengthen your heart,
all ye that hope in the Lord...Psalm 31:24*

We had Evrett home for six days. It was a wonderful six days, but oh how he seemed to struggle every day to breathe, to sleep, and just be comfortable. After six days of struggling, my daughter-in-love called me to tell me she was taking him to the emergency room at the children's hospital. That was something I did not want to hear. My heart just sank. A couple of hours later I got another call with more news I did not want to hear. Evrett was being readmitted to the Pediatric Intensive Care Unit. NO! We just got him home. My daughter-in-love just got to start being a mom to all of her children at the same time. My son just got his wife and son back. The girls just got to start going to bed with their mom, dad, and brother in the same house. I could not even imagine everyone going back to that old routine of the family continually being separated.

I went to the hospital the next day, and when I walked into Evrett's room, I just began weeping at his bedside. I looked at him lying there, and my heart just broke; again. I thought to myself, "How could this possibly be happening? We were supposed to get a miracle, a seven-part creative miracle at that. Evrett was supposed to be healed by now. We waited 115 days just to take him home for six days?" As I stood there by Evrett's bed, I could not imagine the family having to be separated again. When I walked out of his room the look on my daughter-in-love's face expressed that very same dread.

I pulled myself together as I told my daughter-in-love, "We are on a sweet journey. A journey that many people are never blessed enough to be chosen for. We are going to get to see a miracle!" I hugged my daughter-in-love, and I prayed over her, "Father, in the name of Jesus, give my daughter-in-love strength right now. Comfort her and help her through this part of the journey. Bless her with peace knowing that Evrett is healed and all is well."

But if I could pray again...

Most gracious Heavenly Father, I ask that you help my daughter-in-love through your Holy Spirit understand that you have a divine plan for Evrett. Your plan for him includes peace, and not evil because you have intricately ordained a beautiful future for him (Jeremiah 29:11) and nothing about your plan has changed in any way. Sickness has not changed your plan. Doctor's diagnoses have not changed your plan. Hospital stays have not changed your plan. Make known to my daughter-in-love that when you are for us, nothing can stand against us! (Romans 8:31). I pray that you undergird my daughter-in-love and help her to be steadfast, unmovable, always abounding in the work of the Lord, reassuring her that her labor through this journey is not in vain in the Lord! (1 Corinthians 15:58). Let my daughter-in-love take comfort in knowing that she can have peace in you. Even though the storm is raging, even though this battle seems to be endless, and even though there is trouble in this world, she can be of good cheer knowing that you have overcome this world (John 16:33). I pray that you renew her spirit and not let her grow weary in well doing (2 Thessalonians 3:13) knowing that your grace is sufficient to carry her through. Help her to understand that when she is weak she can draw strength from you, and that through her weaknesses the power of Christ will rest upon her (2 Corinthians 12:9). I ask for all these things in the name of Jesus. Amen.

Day 13

The Day the Pain Came

*Let your steadfast love comfort me
according to your promise to your servant...Psalm 119:76 (ESV)*

I was on my way to the hospital to relieve my son and daughter-in-love so they could be at home with the girls for the weekend. I thought this would be a wonderful visit just like every other visit. I would read whatever book I brought with me, stand at Evrett's bed, and tell him how much Gigi loved him. I would hold his hand and if they had him placed just right, I could even lean over the bedrails and kiss his precious head. That was always one of my favorite parts of the visit. However, this would not turn out to be a visit like every other visit.

When I got there I found some literature that had been given to my son and daughter-in-love. Literature from the Palliative Care Team. As I began reading over the literature that had been given to my children my heart began to sink deep inside of me. I lost my breath as I read statements like; given to improve the quality of life for patients who have a serious, chronic, or life-threatening disease. Palliative Care can help make arrangements for long-term care for those with a short life expectancy. Palliative Care can even help with end-of-life arrangements. I began to weep with a deep pain for my children. The doctors had given up on Evrett ever recovering. The doctors had diagnosed my grandson with a life-threatening disease that would affect Evrett's quality of life and length of life. The doctors were preparing my children for the death of their son.

We were having special prayer meetings for Evrett's healing. We were fasting for Evrett's healing. We were taking communion for Evrett's healing. On two occasions, my husband even had our church congregation take part in the Jericho march around our sanctuary in declaration that we were going to see the walls of sickness fall in our precious baby boy. During all of this time, my children were receiving a different declaration, a different report, and taking part in a different battle march. My heart hurt for my children again in a way I had never experienced before. As I laid the literature down I prayed, "My God, my God, help my children!"

But if I could pray again...

Father, I come to you on behalf of my children, and I ask that you bless them and comfort them for they are mourning (Matthew 5:4). Father, you are the Father of mercies and the God of all comfort. You comfort us in all our tribulation (2 Corinthians 1:3-4), and you sent your Son to comfort all that mourn (Isaiah 61:2). I pray right now that my children run into the secret place of the most high and abide under the shadow of the Almighty.

For you, Lord, are their refuge and their fortress: in you they will trust. I thank you, Lord, for delivering my children from the snare of the fowler, and from the noisome pestilence. Thank you for covering my children with your feathers, and under your wings shall my children trust. Your truth shall be their shield and buckler during this attack from the enemy. (Psalm 91:1-4). Thank you, Lord, for comforting my children and for having mercy upon them during this affliction (Isaiah 49:13). Finally, Lord, help my children take comfort in knowing this: that nothing, not this tribulation, not this distress, not this attack, neither death nor life, nor angels nor rulers, nor things present nor things to come, nor powers, nor height nor depth, nor anything else in all creation, will be able to separate them from the love of God in Christ Jesus our Lord. Knowing that in all these things they are more than conquerors through your son, Christ Jesus, who loves them (Romans 8:35, 37-39). I ask for these things in the name of Jesus. Amen.

Day 14

The Day the Death Came

For whether we live, we live unto the Lord; and whether we die, we die unto the Lord: whether we live therefore, or die, we are the Lord's...Romans 14:8

My daughter-in-love was taking Evrett to an appointment with his lung specialist that day. It was supposed to be an appointment to set up a course of action to repair the damage that had been done to Evrett's lungs by his premature birth. My daughter-in-love was actually very hopeful that this specialist was going to get Evrett on the fast track to recovery. It ended up being an appointment which resulted in admitting Evrett back into the Pediatric Intensive Care Unit, once again, with a diagnosis of pneumonia and a bacterial infection.

Evrett had been back in PICU for over a week when Spring Break arrived. I arranged to stay with Evrett for a couple of days at the hospital so my daughter-in-love could go home and spend some time with my son and the girls. She was going to take the girls shopping for Easter dresses, and spend some long overdue quality time with them. I was as happy for my daughter-in-love to leave the hospital as I was for myself to be there. I had been looking forward to spending this time with Evrett. Little did I know what was about to take place.

Late that night Evrett started crying. He was crying so hard that he lost his breath. I am not talking about losing his breath as most babies do when they cry. I am talking about crying until he stopped breathing. Evrett turned the darkest purple I had ever seen. The nurse began shaking and gently squeezing his sides. She turned him in a different direction, and continued to massage his chest. I quietly stood beside his bed watching. The nurse was just about to call for additional assistance when Evrett finally gasped for air and began breathing. Once all of Evrett's vital signs had returned to normal and he had calmed down, I asked the nurse if she would have to call my daughter-in-love and let her know what happened. I so wanted my daughter-in-love to have a break. I wanted her to be able to enjoy some time at home. I knew if the hospital called her she would be restless and second-guessing whether she should have left him. The nurse said that since Evrett had recovered before having to bag him or do chest compressions she would not have to call his mom. I was relieved. My relief was short lived.

Evrett made it through the night without any more complications. He was doing well all morning, so at lunchtime I decided to go to the cafeteria and get something to eat. I then decided to go by the gift shop to get my daughter-in-love a couple of gifts to leave in the room for her to have when she came back to the hospital. That is when I received the call. My daughter-in-love screaming hysterically, "You've got to get back to the room, something is wrong with Evrett!"

When I got back to Evrett's room it was full of doctors, nurses, and social workers. The doctors and nurses were there for Evrett; the social workers were there for me. I walked up to Evrett's bed and he was lying there lifeless. They had a bag on his face breathing for him, and they were doing chest compressions. No response. Evrett was as gray as faded pavement. I could not believe it. I stood there and said to the Lord, "This is not how this is supposed to end. We're supposed to be getting a miracle." However, there were no signs of any miracle at that moment. The respiratory therapist was administering artificial respiration to Evrett. Beside the respiratory therapist was a nurse timing and logging on a sheet of paper each artificial breath accompanied by no vital signs, including no blood pressure. The nurse started shaking his head 'no' and at that moment, I cried out loud, "Jesus, Jesus, Lord we need you!"

But if I could pray again…

Father, in the name of Jesus, I stand boldly and proclaim that death has lost its sting, and the grave has lost its victory (1 Corinthians 15:55) because I am fully persuaded that what you have promised us you are able also to perform (Romans 4:21). You gave me the power to speak death or life (Proverbs 18:21). In the name of Jesus I speak life! My grandson will NOT die but surely live and declare the works of the Lord! (Psalm 118:17). Lord, you have promised us a miracle. Lord, you have promised us that Evrett is healed by your stripes (1 Peter 2:24) and your promises Lord, are yea, and amen unto the glory of God (2 Corinthians 1:20). Not only will my grandson live but you will restore health unto him, and you will heal Evrett of his wounds (Jeremiah 30:17). Not because I say so but because your word says so and forever, O Lord is your word settled in heaven (Psalm 119:89). Amen!

Day 15

The Day the Rage Came

Now may the Lord of peace himself give you peace at all times in every way.
The Lord be with you all...2 Thessalonians 3:16 (ESV)

After I cried, "Jesus, Jesus, Lord we need you!" you could hear every doctor, every nurse, and every social worker hold their breath. Nobody seemed to move. I think everyone was waiting for an official time of death to be called. Instead, we heard, "we have a blood pressure!" The Lord, once again, had moved on our precious baby boy's body. Slowly, Evrett began to breathe again and have vital signs that were strong enough to measure. I thought seeing my grandson lying on that bed lifeless was the worst, most hopeless thing that I could have ever seen. I did not know that something else that seemed almost as hopeless was soon on its way.

By this time, my daughter-in-love was back at the hospital. All of the immediate family had been called and were on their way to the hospital as well. I was in the waiting room with the girls when the social worker showed up to speak to me. Even though my daughter-in-love had made it back to the hospital, we were still waiting on my son to arrive. The social worker was asking me about my son; if we had reached him and if he was on his way to the hospital yet. I thought it was strange that she was asking me so many questions about where my son was until I heard the word 'bypass machine.' Bypass machine? They were waiting for my son to arrive to get parental consent from both parents to hook my grandson up to life-support. I thought seeing my grandson lying on a bed lifeless was the worst, most hopeless thing that I could have ever seen until I saw what it did to my son to see his son lying on a bed lifeless and then being asked to consent for his son to be hooked up to life-support.

My son did not take the news well at all. He did not want to see his son living without any kind of quality of life. He did not want to see his son simply existing on a machine, and that was about as much hope as the doctors were offering at this point. My son just wanted his son to be healthy, to be well, to be healed, and to be home. We were all so focused on Evrett's recovery that we did not even see the devastation and rage that was overtaking my son. While we were all in the waiting room waiting to hear the final decision my son left the hospital. He just could not bear watching what was about to happen to his son. That day something broke in my son. The deep sadness that had turned to anger, the deep heartbreak that had turned to mourning, and the deep desperation that had turned to hopelessness had now ignited into a burning rage. A rage that changed my son in a way I could never have imagined possible. Sadly, I am sure that if I offered any prayer up at all for my son it was something along the lines of, "Lord, help my son not to be so hurt."

But if I could pray again...

Father, I come boldly on behalf of my son and rebuke these winds and command this stormy sea, PEACE BE STILL in the name of Jesus! (Mark 4:39). You are not the author of this confusion. You are the author of peace (1 Corinthians 14:33), and your peace passes all understanding. I pray right now that you keep my son's heart and mind divinely protected through this situation (Philippians 4:7). Lay my son down in peace, make him to sleep in peace, and make him to dwell each day throughout this journey in peace (Psalm 4:8). Let the peace of God rule in my son's heart (Colossians 3:15) and lead my son to seek and pursue peace continually (Psalm 34:14). Father, you promised to give strength to your people and bless your people with peace (Psalm 29:11). I claim this promise for my son right now because the kingdom of God is nothing but righteousness, peace, and joy in the Holy Ghost (Romans 14:17). My son needs your peace right now to wash over his heart, mind, and soul! Thank you for the peace that passes understanding that is being ministered to my son right now in the name of Jesus! Amen.

Day 16

The Day the Second Change Came

*Then they cried unto the LORD in their trouble,
and he delivered them out of their distresses...Psalm 107:6*

My grandson was put on life support for the next three weeks before the next decision would be made. My daughter-in-love was camped out beside him in the hospital, my granddaughters had been moved in with me, and no one really knew where my son was. We all assumed he went home, but no one saw him for a couple of days. He did not go back to the hospital to see his son. He did not come to my house to see his daughters. He did not go to work; he had already quit his job. There was a terrible change taking place in my son.

It was nearly a month before I saw my son again. He was not my son anymore. He did not look the same. He did not act the same. He did not think the same. He did not talk the same. Something happened to my son the day he broke down in the hospital. It affected every part of who he was. We all tried to overlook the changes in him. We, as a family, did not even talk about it for a while. The entire family just covered it over with compassion.

We all agreed that my son was just having a difficult time dealing with what was happening to his own son. I think that we were all just hoping that as Evrett got better my son would get better. Unfortunately, that was not how it was working out.

I was sitting in my office when I got the call from a very concerned family member who asked, "What is going on with your oldest son?" Finally, what we had all been keeping silent about, someone spoke out loud. I just broke down and began crying. I knew my oldest son was not the same person. I knew the enemy had come in and wreaked havoc on my son's heart. I knew that all the pain and heartbreak had changed my son in a significant way. I knew that depression was trying to consume every part of my son's mind, body, and soul. I watched this happen to my son right before my eyes, and I prayed for him. I prayed a weak, defeated, momma-prayer, "Lord have mercy on my son. You know what he is going through, you know his heart is broken, you know how hurt he is; help him, Lord."

But if I could pray again...

Dear Heavenly Father, I speak your word over my son right now because your word heals us and delivers us from destruction (Psalm 107:20). You, Lord, know how to deliver the godly out of temptations and trials; bring your deliverance to my son! (2 Peter 2:9). I recognize right now that this is the work of the adversary, the devil. He is seeking to devour my son but I stand in the gap and resist this attack steadfast in the faith (1 Peter 5:8-9) and ask that you bring my son up out of this horrible pit, out of the miry clay, and set his feet upon the rock and establish him through this part of the journey (Psalm 40:2). Your word declares the devil is a liar and the father of it. I declare these lies spoken to my son concerning his son be exposed (John 8:44). The enemy is trying to blind my son's mind so the light of the glorious gospel of Christ would be hid (2 Corinthians 4:4). I declare that the Holy Spirit reveal the truth to my son. The truth that Evrett is not going to die. The truth that Evrett is not going to be a 'vegetable.' The truth is that we are going to get our miracle because our Lord and Savior has already fought and won this battle against principalities and powers and made a show of them openly, triumphing over them in all things! (Colossians 2:15). Thank you, Lord, for winning this battle for us, and I ask that you reveal that truth to my son right now in Jesus name! Amen.

Day 17

The Day the Isolation Came

*Bear ye one another's burdens,
and so fulfil the law of Christ...Galatians 6:2*

My daughter-in-love and granddaughters had been staying with us since the day my son left the hospital. We set them up a make-shift bedroom in the office. My daughter-in-love would come home every Thursday to spend time with the girls on the weekends. Then, every Sunday she would head back to the hospital to spend the week with Evrett. Sundays were hard on everyone. My granddaughters would cry, my daughter-in-love would cry, and sometimes, I would cry. It was so hard to see everyone so sad day after day, week after week, and month after month. It was so hard to see this precious family living in separation.

After about a month, I came home from work on a Thursday and found that all the girls' clothes and personal items had been packed up and were gone. My daughter-in-love was gone, my granddaughters were gone, and all their things were gone. Without a word, they were just gone. I knew that day that there was another shift taking place. I knew that something was very wrong. I knew that something had happened in my daughter-in-love's heart to make her go, but I did not know what, and I never asked. I knew my daughter-in-love had endured so much heartbreak, pain, fear, and now, with the separation from my son, even loneliness.

I continued to check in everyday with my daughter-in-love like I always did. I never spoke a word about her and the girls leaving. I checked on Evrett, I checked on the girls, and I checked on her, every day. However, things were not the same. Her responses were short. Sometimes she would only send one word responses when I would ask how everyone was doing, "good." Up to this point, my daughter-in-love and I had a wonderful relationship. We were very close, and we talked to each other on a daily basis even before Evrett was born. However, something was very wrong now.

My daughter-in-love began pulling away. I did not hear from her anymore unless I initiated the contact. She did not contact me with updates on Evrett. She did not send me pictures of Evrett. We did not text back and forth scriptures of miracles and promises of God concerning Evrett, and the two precious granddaughters that had spent months with me at my house, I did not see anymore. When I went to the hospital on visits my daughter-in-love was very withdrawn from me, and there was such a silent anger. Another vicious attack of the enemy that was taking place right before my very eyes and I offered up another weak, defeated, momma-prayer, "Lord, give my daughter-in-love strength to handle this journey and heal her of the hurt that is so steadily causing her to grow weary."

But if I could pray again...

Father, in the name of Jesus, I come to you on behalf of my daughter-in-love, and I ask that you comfort her. Comfort her in a way that only you can! I ask that you bring light into her heart and into her spirit. Light her candle and enlighten this dark hour for her. Give her the strength to run through the enemy's troops and leap over this wall of pain and sorrow. Lord, your way on this journey is the perfect way. You are the rock, and you are the one who will gird up my daughter-in-love with strength and guide her steps (Psalm 18:28-32). Lord, I ask that your goodness and mercy follow my daughter-in-love wherever this journey takes her (Psalm 23:6), and that you enlarge her steps right now so that her feet do not slip (Psalm 18:36). Lord, you promised us that you would not leave us comfortless (John 14:18) and all though weeping may endure for the night, joy will come in the morning (Psalm 30:5). Bring morning to my daughter-in-love! Finally, Lord, I ask that she find comfort in your merciful kindness (Psalm 119:76) as she acknowledges you as her rock, her fortress, and her deliverer. For you, Lord, are worthy to be praised! (Psalm 18:2-3). Amen.

Day 18

The Day the Discord and Strife Came

*Behold, how good and how pleasant it is
for brethren to dwell together in unity...Psalm 133:1*

My son had finally returned to the hospital. When he did, he stayed at the hospital for almost two months. He slept on the second floor in the community family room. Night after night and day after day, he stayed at the hospital. His anger and rage had subsided, but he was still not my son. Although he was at the hospital with his wife and son, he was not *with his wife and son.* He was just there. When I went to visit Evrett on this particular day I was not sure if my son would be there. My daughter-in-love did not mention that he was, so I thought he might have made a trip home. This was a day that I have relived in my mind over and over again. A day that I have regretted over and over again. A day that my heart has spent much time weeping in deep remorse for over and over again. A day that I wish I could do over.

My son was sitting in a rocking chair right beside Evrett's bed. As soon as I walked in I said, "Oh I didn't know you were here son." He just nodded at me. I walked up to Evrett's bed and starting telling him that Gigi was here and how much I loved him. Then, I turned to my son and said, "Why are you down here? You need to be at home working. You need to be at home taking care of your daughters. I didn't raise you like this!" Regretfully, I am sure I said numerous other things. When I finished, I turned and looked at my grandson lying on that bed and immediately wished I could have taken all of it back. I have wished that same wish many, many times since that day.

I did not realize until that day how my own anger had been silently growing inside. I was angry with my son. Angry with him for quitting his job. Angry with him for not holding on to our promise of a miracle. Angry that he turned away from the Lord. Angry that he turned away from his wife. Angry that he was angry. All that anger had grown into such discord and strife in our family. As I left the hospital that day I prayed, "Lord, help us! My family is falling apart, and I don't know what to do!"

But if I could pray again...

Dear Heavenly Father, I come to you in the name of Jesus, and I ask that you lead my family into one mind and one accord. Lord, help us to be likeminded and to have the same love in humility, and let us put each other above ourselves (Philippians 2:2-3). Help us to be sympathetic, compassionate, and to show love toward one another during this difficult time (1 Peter 3:8). Lord, I declare your word over my family in 1 Corinthians 1:10: we will agree with one another in what we say, and there will be no divisions among us. I declare that my family will be perfectly united in mind and thought as we travel through this journey. I pray that the Holy Spirit will help each one of us to strive for full restoration. I pray that we would encourage one another, be of one mind, and live in peace knowing that the God of peace is with us through this fiery trial (2 Corinthians 13:11). Help us to make every effort to keep the unity of the Spirit through the bond of peace and to live in harmony with one another (Ephesians 4:3, Romans 12:16) knowing that the God of patience and consolation will grant to us to be likeminded one toward another according to Christ Jesus (Romans 15:5). We need the unity of the Lord in our family right now in the name of Jesus! Amen.

Day 19

The Day the Self-Pity Came

Ye are of God, little children,
and have overcome them (who are not of God);
because greater is he that is in you, than he that is in the world...1
John 4:4

After Evrett was taken off life-support he was put on a paralytic drug in addition to multiple other drugs which kept him continually asleep. Evrett never woke up, and Evrett never moved. Nonetheless, I talked to him just like he could hear me; he could. During this particular visit, I sat at the side of Evrett's bed and read the Bible to him. I would reach up periodically and rub his hand or arm. I would tell him how much I loved him, and then I would continue reading.

For no apparent reason Evrett's heartrate began to increase, and he began having difficulty breathing. The nurse began the regular course of action; checking to see if it was time for his medication again, contacting the charge nurse, and finally, calling a doctor in. While this was going on the nurse also made another call. She called my daughter-in-love. I did not hear the conversation, but

I got the results via a text message which read, "I think Evrett has had enough Gigi time today." It was obvious that the nurse felt like my reading out loud to Evrett and touching his hand caused him this great distress; she passed that opinion on to Evrett's mom. I responded heartbroken, "Ok, I will leave." My daughter-in-love did not want me to leave; she just wanted Evrett to recover.

I sat in a chair for three hours wallowing in self-pity. Thinking, "I can't touch my grandson? I can't read to my grandson? Me sitting by his bed makes him sick? He's been down here how many days and me reading to him is what made him sick? NO! He needs his family here. He needs to hear the word of the Lord! He needs to be loved!" For three solid hours those thoughts raced through my mind over and over and over again. I wanted to scream, "Love does not make a baby sick!" But I didn't. I just sat there, crying most of the time, and feeling sorry for myself. Feeling sorry for Evrett. Feeling sorry for my family. Feeling sorry for the situation. I would say that I wasted three hours when I could have been praying, but self-pity does more than just waste time; it gives the enemy power. Power over one's emotions. Power of one's words. Power over one's actions. I prayed that day. I prayed a prayer of self-pity when I should have been praying all of heaven down upon the enemy's forces!

But if I could pray again...

Father, I recognize right now that my enemy is not flesh and blood. My fight is against principalities, against powers, against the rulers of the darkness of this world, against spiritual wickedness in high places. Therefore, I put on the whole armor of God right now so that I may be able to withstand this evil attack and stand for my faith in you, praying always with all prayer and supplication in the Spirit, and watching thereunto with all perseverance and supplication for my grandson, Evrett (Ephesians 6:12-13, 18). The enemy does not want me to release the power of healing through your spoken word (Proverbs 4:20-22) but I bind the strong man, knowing that you have already spoiled his wicked plan and destroyed the works of the devil which are set against my grandson's recovery (Matthew 12:29, 1 John 3:8). Lord, just as Michael, the archangel, turned to you during a great battle with the devil; I turn to you and declare as Michael did, "Lord, rebuke thee!" (Jude1:9). Rebuke this attack from the enemy in the name of Jesus and begin to release your favor upon our family! For you bless the righteous, O Lord; you cover him with favor as with a shield (Psalm 5:12). Put a shield of divine favor around Evrett and keep him protected by your shield in the name of Jesus! Amen.

Day 20

The Day the Separation Came

And the LORD God said, It is not good that the man should be alone;
I will make him an help meet for him...Genesis 2:18

My daughter-in-love had confided in me that she did not know how much more of her broken marriage she would be able to endure. She wanted things to be different. She wanted my son to be different. She wanted her marriage to be different. She wanted her life to be different. She tried to focus on taking care of Evrett and the girls, and hoped for different. Different did not come.

I was at home when I got the call from my daughter-in-love. "I wanted you to know that I am going to file for divorce." My heart, once again, fell to the very pit of my stomach, and I felt physically sick. I softly replied, "I wish there was something I could do to help." She said, "I wish there was something someone could do to help." I heard and felt the desperation in my daughter-in-love's voice that day. Her life, her marriage, and her hope appeared to be slipping away, and there did not seem to be anything anyone could do to help her. I did not blame my daughter-in-love, but I hurt deeply for my son that day.

My son did not realize what the enemy was trying to steal from him. My son did not realize that the enemy has no mercy. My son did not realize that the enemy was not only after him, but the enemy was after his entire family. My heart was so heavy that day. I began weeping for my daughter-in-love. I began weeping for my granddaughters. I began weeping for my son. I was watching the devil destroy my son's family right before my eyes, and I did not know what to do to help. So, I prayed, "Lord, help my son to see what is going on. Help my son to realize what the devil is doing to his family. Take the scales off my son's eyes before it's too late!"

But if I could pray again...

Dear Heavenly Father, I declare a marriage blessing over my children in the name of Jesus! You ordained marriage from the beginning and declared that marriage is honorable and that whoso findeth a wife finedeth a good thing, and obtaineth favor of the Lord! (Hebrews 13:4, Proverbs 18:22). I speak your favor to shine upon my children's marriage right now and pray that you strengthen their marriage through the bond of the Holy Spirit. You honor a man who for the cause of the marriage covenant shall leave his father and mother, and shall cleave to his wife: and they two shall be one flesh. Wherefore my children are no more two, but one flesh. What therefore God hath joined, let not man put asunder. No man, no trial, no hardship, no hurt, no anger; nothing shall separate the love my children have for one another! (Matthew 19:4-6). I declare that my son loves his wife as Christ loves the church, and my son will give himself to his wife as Christ gave himself to the church (Ephesians 5:25) and in turn, my daughter-in-love will reverence my son as she reverences the Lord (Ephesians 5:33). With all lowliness and meekness, with longsuffering, and forbearance, my children will love one another (Ephesians 4:2). My daughter-in-love looks well to the ways of her household, and because of this her husband will call her blessed and praise her (Proverbs 31:27-28). I declare the everlasting love of the Lord and his lovingkindness (Jeremiah 31:3) to cover this marriage and bind this union together for the duration of this beautiful journey called life! In the name of Jesus, I declare it so! Amen.

Day 21

The Day the Desperation Came

And God said, "Let there be light," and there was light...
Genesis 1:3 (NIV)

Evrett had been kept paralyzed and asleep for almost three months now. I knew the doctors would soon make a decision as to what the next course of action should be. I knew the doctors were not going to continue with this same course of treatment inevitably. My daughter-in-love had shared with me that they had a family meeting planned the following afternoon with all the doctors involved with Evrett's case. They were going to discuss possible treatments for his further recovery. As always, I told her to keep me updated.

It was 8:00 p.m. the following evening and I still had not heard from my daughter-in-love. I sent her a text and asked her if she had met with all of Evrett's doctors. I soon understood why she had not contacted me. The doctors had told my daughter-in-love that they were going to give Evrett 30 days to show some sort of improvement. At the end of 30 days if there were no signs of improvement Evrett would be taken off all medical support. I called her as soon as I read her text. My daughter-in-love was crushed. Her voice was different, and her words were different. She had just been given a death sentence for her son. She had just been told, "You have 30 days left to be a mom to your son." My daughter-in-love was distraught. She was at a place emotionally that was lower than I had ever seen her.

There were no words that day. What do you say to a mom who was just told that her son was probably going to die? What do you say to a mom who just heard, "We've done everything medically possible, and there just doesn't seem to be any signs of recovery"? I prayed that day for the Lord to give my daughter-in-love peace and comfort.

But if I could pray again...

Father, I speak light into my daughter-in-love's mind and heart right now. Your Son, Jesus, was sent to be the light of all mankind. Your word declares that Jesus is the light that shines in the darkness, and the darkness has not overcome him. I claim this promise for my daughter-in-love; she will NOT be overcome by this darkness! (John 1:4-5). I claim the promises of the word that because of the tender mercy of our God, we have been sent a rising sun that will come to us from heaven to shine on those living in darkness and in the shadow of death, to guide our feet into the path of peace (Luke 1:78-79). I speak the light of Jesus into this situation. Shine on this shadow of death and guide my daughter-in-love into the path of peace! You are the light of this world, and I pray my daughter-in-love follows after you because you have promised that if she does, she will never walk in darkness but will have the light of life (John 8:12). Father, you have promised to let light shine out of the darkness. I claim that promise for my daughter-in-love. I ask that you make your light shine in her heart to give her the light of the knowledge of God's glory that is displayed in the face of Christ (2 Corinthians 4:6). Destroy this darkness by your light! Reveal to my daughter-in-love that in this moment of darkness the enemy is trying to consume her with, that she has been called out of the darkness into the marvelous light of Jesus Christ (1 Peter 2:9). Finally, Lord, I ask that you give her strength to cast off the works of this darkness and help her to put on the armor of light! (Romans 13:12). I ask that you cover my daughter-in-love in the light of your dear Son, Jesus Christ! Amen.

Day 22

The Day the Reality Came

*Put on the whole armour of God,
that ye may be able to stand against the wiles of the
devil...Ephesians 6:11*

It had been almost nine months since the journey first began. During those nine months I literally watched my family fall apart right before my very eyes. I watched my children leave the church we pastor. I watched my son turn away from the Lord, and lay down his calling in the music ministry. I watched hurt, anger, and depression try to consume my children. I watched my son and daughter-in-love's marriage deteriorate. I watched my son die inside. I watched my children watch their dreams shatter. I watched my relationship with daughter-in-love grow distant and cold. I watched discord and strife affect other relationships within our family. I just stood by and watched this happen. I watched it happen, and I did nothing.

I am supposed to be the spiritual matriarch of my family. I have been born-again for 27 years. I have been filled with the baptism of the Holy Ghost for 25 years. I co-pastor a church with my husband. I am called to teach and preach the gospel. I have a foundation of faith. I know the promises of God. I believe those promises are for me and my family. I believe in healing. I believe in the delivering power of the name of Jesus. I believe greater is he who is in me than he who is in this world. So, why did I just stand by watching what was happening and seemly do nothing?

When this reality hit me, I began to weep deeply. How could I let this happen to my family? I knew it was happening. I watched it happen, and I let it happen. My children were under a fierce attack from the enemy, and I did not declare war! I willingly surrendered. I saw what the enemy was doing, and I stood by and allowed it to happen without travailing in intercessory prayer for my children! I fell on my face and cried out to the Lord, "Why didn't I do anything? Why did I let this happen?"

But if I could pray again...

Father, in the name of Jesus, if I could do it all over again I would declare war! Spiritual war, knowing that though we walk in the flesh, we do not war after the flesh: for the weapons of our warfare are not carnal, but mighty through God to the pulling down of strong holds. I pull down every strong hold of sickness and disease attacking my grandson. I pull down the strongholds of depression, heartbreak, anger, and hopelessness that are attacking my children. I cast down imaginations and every high thing that exalteth itself against the knowledge of God, and bring into captivity every thought to the obedience of Christ. Every lie the devil attacks my children with concerning the healing of their son is cast down and rendered powerless in the name of Jesus (2 Corinthians 10:3-5). The enemy who has risen up against us will be defeated before us according to the promise in Deuteronomy 28:7 because the demons must submit to the name of Jesus! Jesus declared it to be so when he told the disciples, "I saw Satan fall like lightning from heaven. I have given you authority to trample on snakes and scorpions and to overcome all the power of the enemy; nothing will harm you" (Luke 10:17-19). My God, my God, at the power we have over the enemy in Jesus name! I execute that power right now, I resist this attack of the enemy, and I command the devil to flee from my children and my grandson (James 4:7). Furthermore, I release the promise of Matthew 18:18 when Jesus said, "Whatsoever ye shall bind on earth shall be bound in heaven: and whatsoever ye shall loose on earth shall be loosed in heaven." I bind the enemy forces. I bind sickness and disease. I bind the tormenting lies of the devil. I bind the spirit of fear, and in the name of Jesus I loose the truth, knowing that the truth will set my children and my grandson free! (John 8:32). We have a promise, and I claim it right now: no weapon that is formed against us shall prosper, and every tongue that shall rise against us in judgment thou shalt condemn. This is the heritage of the servants of the Lord, and their righteousness is of me, saith the Lord (Isaiah 54:17). I speak with boldness 1 John 5:4-5: For me and my children, and my grandson are born of God and whatsoever is born of God overcometh the world, and this is the victory that overcometh the world, even our faith. Who is he that overcometh the world, but he that believeth that Jesus is the Son of God? We are believers in Jesus, the Son of God, therefore; we are overcomers! My children will overcome this trial. My children will overcome this heartbreak. My children will overcome this anger and hurt because Jesus has already destroyed him that had the power of death, that is, the devil (Hebrews 2:14). Our faith in the name of Jesus will make us overcomers in all of this! Amen.

Then, the Lord spoke to my heart and said, "Start praying, like you COULD pray again." So from that moment on, every morning I would get up early, enter my prayer closet, and pray for my children as I wished I would have from the beginning.

Day 23

The Day the Decision Came

*Praise the Lord! Oh give thanks to the Lord,
for he is good, for his steadfast love endures forever!
Psalm 106:1 (ESV)*

Evrett was almost 11 months old now and had spent all but about six weeks of his life in the hospital. I went to see Evrett right before school was getting ready to start in August. I spent quite a while with him that day. It was a wonderful visit. He was wide-awake for the first part of the visit. I told him how much we all loved him and how much everyone missed him. I told him that poppa was ready for him to come home so they could go fishing together. I told him that his sisters were ready for him to come home so they could hold him, and I told him that his mommy and daddy were ready for him to come home so they could all be together. I did not know that would be the last time I would be able to see my grandson.

I got the call from my daughter-in-love the week after school started. She told me that Evrett could no longer have any visitors. Since school started there were concerns about so many germs being passed around. It was just too dangerous to risk Evrett contracting a virus. My heart sank deep into the pit of my stomach as I thought, "I can't see my grandson? I can't talk to him? I can't hold his hand? I can't tell him how much I love him?" Just when I thought my heart could not be broken into more than a million pieces, it broke into a million and one pieces. I could not imagine no more visits. No more kisses. No more pictures. No more talks. No more nothing.

If that news was not upsetting enough, the reality of missing my grandson's first birthday was the final blow. Now, my heart was in one million and two tiny, little, broken pieces. I would not be able to see my grandson the day he turned one. I would not be able to sing happy birthday to Evrett on his first birthday. I would not be able to take pictures of him on his first birthday. I would not be there on his first birthday. I so desperately wanted my grandson to come home. I so desperately wanted my children home, together. I so desperately prayed, "Lord, finish healing Evrett so he doesn't have to spend his second birthday in the hospital!"

But if I could pray again...

Father, in the name of Jesus, I thank you for the seven part creative miracle you are doing in Evrett. Thank you for the missing third part of his brain that you have given back to him. Thank you for his new lungs that are healthy and can breathe. Thank you for his perfect vision and hearing and his ability to eat. Thank you that Evrett can wrap his arms and legs around his mommy and daddy and say, "I LOVE YOU!" I will sing unto you and talk of all your wondrous works (1 Chronicles 16:9). I will remember your wondrous works which you have done (1 Chronicles 16:12). I will praise my God, who does great things, unfathomable and wondrous works without number (Job 9:10), God thunders with his wondrous voice, God does awesome works that we do not comprehend (Job 37:5). Lord, I will publish with my voice of thanksgiving, and tell of all thy wondrous works (Psalm 26:7). I will shout, blessed be the Lord God, the God of Israel, who only does wondrous things (Psalm 72:18). I will not conceal your wondrous works, but I will tell them to the generation to come (Psalm 78:4). I will give thanks unto Jehovah for his loving-kindness and for his wondrous works to the children of men (Psalm 107:8). I will speak of the glorious honor of thy majesty and of thy wondrous works (Psalm 145:5). To the one who alone does great and wondrous things, for his gracious love is everlasting, I will praise you (Psalm 136:4). Thank you, Lord, for healing my grandson! Amen.

Day 24

The Day the Holy Spirit Came

But ye, beloved, building up yourselves on your most holy faith, praying in the Holy Ghost...Jude 1:20

I had been getting up earlier every morning and entering my prayer closet to intercede for my son and daughter-in-love before going to work for several weeks now. I had made up my mind up that I would not surrender this battle. The devil could not have my children. The enemy was not going to destroy my family because I was not going to let it happen!

Every morning I would enter that closet, get on my face before the Lord, and begin crying out for my children. I would bind the spirit of depression and anger. I would call out for the Lord to heal their broken hearts and give them peace and comfort. I would pray blessings down on my children. I would ask the Lord to increase their hope and give them an overwhelming desire to read their Bibles so their faith would ever increase in strength. Day after day, for weeks, I would call out to the Lord, "my children need this, help my children with this, they need..." and then one day I just stopped praying and I began to cry uncontrollably as I said, "Lord, how can I possibly know what my children need. I don't know what they need. Only you, Lord, know of the deep wounds and the hidden hurts. Only you, Lord, know how to heal my children's hearts and minds."

But if I could pray again...

Father, I do not know how to effectively pray for my children. I do not know the inner most parts of their hearts, their hurts, their fears, or their disappointments but you do. Therefore, Lord, I turn to your Holy Spirit in prayer knowing that the Spirit will minister to the deep wounds of my children's hearts. I know the Spirit will search my children's heart and make intercession for my children according to the will of God in this situation (Romans 8:26-27). I commit my children to you Lord, and with all prayer and supplication in the Spirit, I pray for them with all perseverance and supplication (Ephesians 6:18). And so it began, a deep intercession in the Spirit for my children...Arise, cry out in the night, at the beginning of the night watches! Pour out your heart like water before the presence of the Lord! Lift your hands to him for the lives of your children (Lamentations 2:19). In the name of Jesus! Amen.

Day 25

The Day the Love Came

God is love...1 John 4:8

It was a Sunday morning service and I had been in pre-service prayer like every other Sunday morning. The worship service had started but I do not remember what song was being sung. All I can remember is that I was standing on the stage when an intense heat started running through my body on the inside. The heat was so hot that it made me feel physically faint. I closed my eyes, and when I did I saw myself standing in a bright, yellow light, and rain was falling on me. All around me was gray, but there I stood in the bright, yellow light with a consistent, steady rain falling on me. I stood there in perfect peace, completely quiet, and totally still. I was not praying. I was not fasting. I was not reading my Bible. I was just standing there totally still. I was not sad. I was not angry. I was not hurt. I was just standing there in a bright, yellow light with rain falling on me completely quiet, and in perfect peace. I spent the next several days praying about what I had seen. I knew there had to be a significant meaning to what I had experienced.

Almost two weeks had went by before the Lord revealed to me the meaning of what I had seen. I was sitting on the couch in the living room reading a book about the Holy Spirit and revival. I began crying, and I could feel the Holy Spirit sweeping over me. I began to feel the love of Jesus as I had never felt it before in my entire life. It washed over me like floodwaters. Just washing all of the pain, hurt, and anger out of me, off of me, and away from me. A love so perfect and so holy it was just amazing. The spirit of the Lord showed me that the rain I saw falling on me was the love of Jesus. I began to understand that the love of Jesus is a powerful force that can heal and restore life to the deepest, most broken parts of a person's heart. I began to understand that the love of Jesus can bring perfect peace to a person no matter what they have went through. I began to understand that the love of Jesus can wash away years of pain, hurt, anger, and depression in just a moment's time.

Then the Spirit of the Lord spoke ever so softly these words to my heart, "The love of Jesus is what will heal your son and your daughter-in-love." I knew that day that all my children needed was the love of Jesus. The perfect, pure, and holy love of Jesus was the answer I had been so earnestly searching for. I had been praying for strength, peace, comfort, and healing for my children.

But If I could pray again...

Father, in the name of Jesus, I ask that you cover my children in your love. Let them feel your love flood their hearts and minds to the core of their very being. Reveal to my children the truth of your love; your love is patient and kind. Your love holds no anger. Your love does not hold our sins against us. Your love will protect my children. Your love will give my children hope. Your love will preserve my children, and your love will never fail my children! (1 Corinthians 13:4-8). Lord, my children need your love. If your love is powerful enough to cover a multitude of sins (1 Peter 4:8), I know most assuredly, that it is powerful enough to heal this hurt and brokenness in my children's hearts! Shine your perfect love that casteth out all fear upon my children (1 John 4:18). More than faith and more than hope, my children need your love (1 Corinthians 16:14). The love that led you to the cross to lay down your life for us, I ask that you pour out upon my children right now! (John 15:13). Amen.

Day 26

The Day the Weeping Came

And when the Lord saw her, he had compassion on her, and said unto her, Weep not...Luke 7:13

It started one day during my morning prayer time. I began to weep. I felt a flood of emotions rush over me that hurt my heart so intensely that all I could do was weep. My heart was weeping for my son and my daughter-in-love. My heart hurt so deeply and so sorrowfully that I began to realize that must be the pain in my son's heart. That hurt me even more. I could do nothing but weep. I tried to stop crying. I tried to pull myself together but to no avail. The weeping continued. When I realized how deeply my son had been hurting and how I had not done anything to reach out to him; I completely broke down. I called my husband crying so uncontrollably that all I could do while sobbing was cry out, "I should have went to my son in love, not anger. I should have helped my son with this hurt. I should have prayed with my son. I should have told my son that I was concerned about him. I should have prayed the love of Jesus over my son, into my son, and around son!" My husband tried to console me, but I just kept saying over and over again, "My son needed the love of Jesus, and I didn't show it to him. I didn't go to him in love. I didn't pray with him in love. I didn't talk to him in love. I waited too long, and then I went to him in anger. Oh, my God, what have I done?"

I would like to say that the weeping soon subsided but it did not. It got worse. I then began to weep for my daughter-in-love. I thought back to the day she was so distraught over the initial report concerning her unborn son. She wanted someone she could turn to, someone she could share her deepest concerns and worst fears with, someone who would cry with her. I would not be that person. I would not cry with her. I had to be strong. I had to have faith. I had to speak the word. My daughter-in-love told me that she needed me to be a mom right then, not her pastor, not a faith teacher, just a mom. I cried out to my husband once again, "All she wanted was for me to cry with her and I wouldn't do it! I should have cried with her. I wasn't there for her like she needed me to be!"

After two or three hours the tears were all gone, but the weeping only stopped temporarily. Every day during my prayer time for my children I would weep uncontrollably. Sometimes while I was getting ready for work I would begin to weep. Sometimes while at work I would begin to weep. Sometimes while I was cooking, cleaning, driving, eating, it really did not matter, just sometimes, for weeks on end, I would begin to weep. I would weep for what my children were going through, and I would weep for what I did and did not do. Every time I would weep I would pray, "Oh Lord, why didn't I do anything to help my children. Why did I just let this happen?"

But if I could pray again...

Father, I come to you in a spirit of humility. Lord, you know my heart. I tried to be so careful not to break down in front of my children because I was afraid that if they saw me weeping, they would think that I had lost faith in our miracle. I realize now that me weeping with my children and for my children is not a sign of my lack of faith. For Jesus himself wept when he saw the grief of Mary and the other Jews over the death of Lazarus (John 11:33-35). My heart is broken, Lord. I hurt for my children in a way that I have never hurt before. Lord, I regret not weeping with my daughter-in-love. If I could do it all over again I would weep with her, and I would mourn with her (Ecclesiastes 3:4). I wish I had stopped long enough to suffer with my children. I wish I would have cried, wept, and mourned with them so they would not have felt so all alone on this journey (1 Corinthians 12:25-26). In the midst of these troubles, many and bitter, restore me, O Lord, and restore my children, in Jesus name. (Psalm 71:20). Amen.

While I Was...

While I was trying to tell my daughter-in-love and my firstborn son,

Hold on to God, keep the faith, and never, never give up.

In spite of what all the doctors say, our miracle is on the way,

"All is well," I would continually proclaim.

While day after day I watched my children's hearts break,

I refused to admit it was almost more than my own heart could take.

"We have a promise," I would say,

"We're getting a miracle, that has not changed!"

While I watched the days turn to weeks, then months, and now a year,

All the while in front of my children, I tried never to shed a tear.

For I must remain rooted and grounded, strong, and full of faith,

Who would be there to help my children, if my very own heart were to break?

While every day I tried to share hope and encouraging words that weren't enough,

I watched depression; anger, sadness, and pain try to consume the ones that I love.

Until my voice grew softer and softer and those I love seemed so far away,

That no one was there to hear my cry, "Our miracle is still on the way!"

So now I have to realize that while I was busy being so strong,

My heart broke into many pieces by watching all that went so wrong.

A mom should be able to help her children and hold her grandson in her arms,

Oh Lord, for that promise of our miracle, so earnestly do I long!

Day 27

The Day the Forgiveness Came

He hath not dealt with us after our sins;
nor rewarded us according to our iniquities...Psalm 103:10

The weeping had turned into a deep brokenness. I had been crying for days. My time in prayer for my children had been changing me. My time in prayer for my children had been exposing my own deep sadness, my own hurt, my own brokenness, my own anger, and my own regrets. Until now, I did not even realize what had been happening to me. I could not put into words the depth of my brokenness, so I just cried. Every morning, every afternoon, every night. I just cried. I cried because of what my children were going through. I cried because of what my grandchildren were going through. I cried because of what my family was going through. I cried because I did not show the love of Jesus to my son as I should have. I cried because of the separation in the relationship between me and my daughter-in-love. I cried because my children were separated, and I cried because all of the brokenness seemed to separate my entire family.

Then I remembered that love. That love that swept over me in my living room that day. That love that is powerful enough to wash away the deepest pain, the darkest sorrow, the most intense anger, and even bring forgiveness to the most hurtful situations. I realized that was what was happening to me through the weeping. The love of Jesus was washing me clean. The love of Jesus was washing away all of the brokenness inside of me. The love of Jesus was healing me of all the regrets of what I did and did not do. The love of Jesus was bringing forgiveness to me so I could forgive myself.

I went to my son and daughter-in-love, and I asked them to forgive me. I told them that I was sorry for not being there for them the way they needed me to be. I told my son that I was sorry that I did not come to him in love and talk to him about what he was feeling and how it was affecting him. I told him that I was sorry for not praying with him and helping him through his darkest hours. I told my daughter-in-love that I was sorry for not being the mom she needed to be and crying with her when she needed me to. I told her that I was sorry for whatever it was that had separated our relationship. Finally, I told them both how much I loved them. When I left that day I prayed, "Lord, I ask that my children receive the love that I have for them both. Restore our family!"

But if I could pray again...

Father, thank you for sending your Son to shed his blood for us for the forgiveness of sins (Matthew 26:28). We have redemption through the blood of Jesus, the forgiveness of sins, according to the riches of his grace

(Ephesians 1:7). When Jesus said, "Father, forgive them, for they know not what they do," he made it possible for us to forgive others (Luke 23:34). For we have all sinned, and come short of the glory of God (Romans 3:23) so help us to be forgiving towards each other. Release the power of the love of Jesus and the healing virtue of forgiveness upon my family. We confess that we have all been hurt, angry, disappointed, desperate, and broken; cleanse us from all unrighteousness (1 John 1:9). Help us to forgive each other just as our heavenly Father has forgiven us (Matthew 6:15). Thank you, Lord, for the gift of forgiveness! I ask that each one of my family members receive this gift in the name of Jesus. Amen.

Day 28

The Day the Faith Came

For we walk by faith, not by sight...2 Corinthians 5:7

I cannot tell you the exact date on the calendar, or the day of the week, or what time of day it was but one day; faith came! What a glorious day it was! You will know when faith comes because peace comes, rest comes, joy comes, contentment comes, confidence comes, comfort comes, certainty comes, trust comes, and reassurance comes!

Now, you must understand that faith is believing without seeing. Faith comes to your heart, your mind, and your soul without you having to see any evidence in this natural world. Faith is, believing so strongly that something exists without there being any evidence whatsoever, without seeing it, without hearing it, without touching it. Nothing had really changed in our natural circumstances. Evrett was still in the hospital on a ventilator, with a feeding tube, and not able to sit up, crawl, suck, swallow, or talk. However, that is not how my heart saw Evrett. My heart saw Evrett well, whole, healed, complete, and restored! I talked about Evrett coming home. I talked about how good Evrett was doing. I talked about poppa taking Evrett fishing. I talked about Evrett riding a bicycle and preaching the word of God because that is how Evrett will be when the seven part creative miracle is manifested completely!

The doctor's reports had no bearing on my mind, my heart, or my emotions. No diagnosis or prognosis could make me fearful because my trust was in knowing that Evrett was going to receive his miracle! No delay, regression, or set back of any kind in Evrett's recovery disappointed me or moved me in any way. Regardless of what the doctors thought, regardless of what people thought, regardless of how it appeared to be to the natural eye, my grandson was going to come home. My grandson was going to walk, talk, go to school, play with his sisters, and share his story with the world!

When faith comes, you cannot talk a person out of it. You cannot convince a person with faith that something will never happen when the promises of God declare that something will happen! You cannot convince a person with faith to look at the natural circumstances around them and accept the reality of what they see. Faith does not see natural circumstances. Faith only sees the promise. While the winds might be boisterous and the storm might be fierce, faith will command the storm, "Peace, be still!" When faith comes it will only believe the report of the Lord. You cannot convince faith of the natural facts; faith only sees the truth of what God has promised! Faith does not see what is, faith sees what will be! I prayed for faith in the early weeks of Evrett's life.

But if I could pray again...

Father, I come boldly before you, declaring the words of your Son, Jesus Christ. Your Son told me to have the faith of God and speak unto this mountain, be thou removed and be cast into the sea. Your Son said that if I do not doubt in my heart, but believe when I speak to that mountain, that it WILL come to pass. Your Son said that what things so ever I desire, when I pray, believe that I receive them, and I shall have them! (Mark 11:22-24). I speak to the mountain of sickness and disease that has attacked my grandson, and I demand that it be removed and cast into the sea. I believe that by the name of Jesus that mountain of sickness and disease MUST move! I will receive what I have desired and prayed for because I believe that your word is true! I do not have to see to believe (Hebrews 11:1). I believe because your word says that it is so! My faith does not stand on a doctor's report or seeing a natural improvement in Evrett's condition; my faith stands in the power of God! (1 Corinthians 2:5). I have come to understand that the only fight in this world is the fight of faith and I have fought a good fight and kept the faith to believe for the completion of Evrett's miracle (2 Timothy 4:7) and because of this, I have entered into the rest that God provides the very moment in time that faith comes! (Hebrews 4:3). In Jesus name, I declare Evrett healed because with God nothing is impossible! (Luke 1:37). Amen.

Day 29

The Day the Restoration Came

And he said unto me, Son of man, can these bones live? And I answered,
O Lord God, thou knowest...Ezekiel 37:3

We had been on this journey for over a year. It had been several months since I had started my early morning prayer time for my children. During this time I rarely saw my son or daughter-in-love, and when I did they were not together. However, this time was different. They were together. Not only were they together, but they were talking to each other, interacting with each other and smiling at each other. It was pure joy to my soul! The relief, the happiness, the hopefulness, and the deep thankfulness I felt that day is almost indescribable. Words really cannot do justice to the overwhelming gratitude I felt toward my Lord and Savior!

I knew the hand of the Lord had been moving in the midst of the situation. I knew the Spirit of the Lord had been healing my children's hearts, and I knew the love of the Lord was bringing restoration to my entire family! That day I saw the evidence of what I had been hoping for! On my way home I prayed, "Lord, thank you so much for what you are doing in my children, and what you are doing for my family!"

But if I could pray again...

Father, thank you for your continual guidance throughout this journey. Thank you for satisfying my children's souls in this drought so they shall be like a watered garden, and like a spring of water, whose water faileth not! (Isaiah 58:11). Lord, I declare the works of Joel 2:25-26 to come upon my children's life: restore what the enemy has tried to steal from my children and their family, and let my children praise the name of the Lord for dealing wondrously with them! I declare the blessing of the double upon my children, and that everlasting joy shall be unto them (Isaiah 61:7). Lord, you have promised that when we turn to you there will be a time of refreshing which will come from your presence (Acts 3:19). Pour out the time of refreshing upon my son and daughter-in-love today! Father, I thank you for this restoration, reconciliation, peace, and comfort that comes to us through your Son, Jesus Christ! Amen.

Day 30

The Day the Miracle Came

*And whatsoever ye shall ask in my name,
that will I do, that the Father may be glorified in the Son...John
14:13*

From the beginning of this journey we were promised a seven part creative miracle. We have seen several parts of the miracle manifested over the past fifteen months. We have seen our baby boy live when he was supposed to die. We have seen our baby boy see and hear when he was supposed to be blind and deaf. We have seen our baby boy think and mimic other people's actions when he was not supposed to have the ability to do so. We have seen our baby boy surpass every expectation the doctors never imagined would be possible for him. However, we have not seen it all. There is still more of this creative miracle to come.

One day we will see the complete manifestation of what God has promised us from the beginning. We will see a total restoration and a miraculous healing take place. We will see Evrett "take up his bed and walk!" I have prayed many times, "Heavenly Father, I know that there is nothing too hard for you (Jeremiah 32:27). You healeth all our diseases! (Palm 103:3). It does not matter how many things have attacked Evrett's body; your word declares that you heal them all! I am a believer, and Jesus said that these signs would follow them that believe, they shall lay hands on the sick, and they shall recover (Mark 16:17-18). Jesus not only has commissioned believers to go forth and lay hands on the sick, but he also gave us the power to heal all manner of sickness and all manner of disease! (Mathew 10:1). Lord, I pray that you grant unto me, thy servant, that with all boldness I will speak your word by stretching forth my hand to heal my grandson; and that signs and wonders may be done in Evrett by the name of your holy child Jesus! (Acts 4:29-30). I believe and therefore shall I see! Amen.

But if I could pray again...

Father, I come to you in the name of Jesus, and call those things which are not as though they were (Romans 4:17): Thank you for the complete manifestation of the seven part creative miracle in my grandson! IT IS FINISHED!

Day 31

The Day the Salvation Came

*Jesus answered him, "Truly, truly, I say to you,
unless one is born again he cannot see the kingdom of God...*
John 3:3 (ESV)

The greatest miracle a person can ever receive is the miracle of salvation; being born again. Receiving salvation is quite simple. Romans 10:9-10 gives us clear instructions on how to receive Jesus as our personal Savior...if you shall confess with your mouth that Jesus is Lord and believe in your heart that God raised him from the dead, you will be saved. For with the heart man believes unto righteousness and with the mouth, confession is made unto salvation. If you have never received the miracle of the new birth in Christ Jesus, I would like to pray with you right now. Pray this prayer with me...

Father, I confess with my mouth that your Son, Jesus Christ, is Lord. I believe that Jesus died on the cross to pay for my sins so I would not have to. I believe that you raised him from the dead on the third day, and I receive and confess that Jesus is my personal Savior.

If you prayed that prayer then you have just been born again. You are a new creature in Christ Jesus; old things are passed away and behold all things have become new (2 Corinthians 5:17). You have just started a new life. A life with Jesus is the best life you will ever know. If you do not have a Bible, get one. You need to begin to fill your new mind and new heart with a new word, the word of God. All of the answers to the questions you have can be found in God's word. His word is a lamp unto your feet and a light unto your path (Psalm 119:105). Now that you are born again I would like to pray for you.

If I could pray again...

Father, I pray right now that your Holy Spirit guide this brother/sister into all truth (John 16:13). Lead them into the truth of your word and lead them to find Christian fellowship in a Bible based church so they can grow in their relationship with you. (1 Thessalonians 5:11, Hebrews 10:25). Father, your word records that there is joy in the presence of the angels of God over one sinner that repents (Luke 15:10); I joy with the angels over this soul that has turned their life over to you! I declare abundant blessings upon their new life in the name of Jesus! Amen.

Evrett's Story

Evrett was born September 5, 2017, at 33 weeks; however, he had stopped growing at 27 weeks. Evrett only weighed 3 lbs. and 4 oz., but that was more than his projected birth weight of 2 lbs. 9 oz. Evrett was so tiny. His entire body could be covered by one of my hands. He wore micro-premi diapers, and they even had to be folded down in half. The smallest premi pacifier the nurse could find covered his entire face when he would suck on it. He was literally skin and bones. You could see every one of his ribs, and his fingers resembled toothpicks. He was so tiny.

Evrett was born with severe hydrocephalus due to the missing third part of his brain. The doctors estimated that half a pound of his weight was from the fluid on his brain. We had been told that Evrett would probably be blind, deaf, have very limited motor skills, if any, and that is all in addition to 'if he survives.' We were told that Evrett had sustained a stroke while still in the womb and there was a suspected mass on his brain. After Evrett was born, the mass would be tested to find out if it was malignant or benign. However, our first round of creative miracles were already being manifested. Evrett did survive. Evrett is not blind. Evrett is not deaf. Evrett did not have a mass of any kind on his brain. Evrett was tested for Down syndrome: negative, and all other chromosomal abnormalities: negative.

After Evrett's birth, he was then diagnosed with Dandy-Walker Malformation, which caused the hydrocephalus due to the missing part of his brain. Evrett was also diagnosed with chronic lung disease and an untreatable heart defect. At six weeks old, Evrett had neurosurgery to place a shunt to drain the fluid off his brain. At three months old, the doctors determined that the amount of energy that it took for sucking and swallowing to drink from a bottle was just too hard on Evrett's lungs, so Evrett had his second surgery. A G-tube was placed in his stomach to feed him.

After 115 days in NICU, Evrett came home for the first time. However, six days later he was readmitted to the hospital, and spent the next week in PICU. Evrett then returned home for the second time, but he did not stay at home very long that time either. On March 8, 2018, Evrett was readmitted to the PICU for pneumonia and a bacterial infection in his lungs. On March 23, he went into cardiac arrest and was put on total life support. Evrett remained on life support for the next week and a half. After being taken off life support, for the next three months, Evrett remained on a paralytic drug and under complete sedation. The doctors at this point had given up on Evrett ever recovering. This led to the decision to begin taking Evrett off the paralytic drug; a drug that one doctor said Evrett would never be able to live without. But he did! Evrett came off that drug and out of that sedated state with the Lord's hand and blessing all over him!

On June 14, Evrett had his third surgery, a tracheotomy. This was done so the vent tubes could go through his neck instead of through his nose. For the first time in Evrett's life we were able to see his face without tubes or medical tape! Once he recovered from that surgery the next phase of drug weaning began. Not only had Evrett been on a paralytic drug for over three months, but he had also been on narcotics for sedation for over three months. So many narcotics that we were told it would take six months to wean him off the drugs safely. During this time Evrett began having seizures and was moved back into the PICU for testing and observation. The doctors never did determine what caused the seizures and the weaning process started back shortly after the seizures subsided.

Not only has Evrett been weaned off the narcotics, the doctors also began weaning him off the ventilator. As of the writing of this book, Evrett's lungs are healthier than they have been since his birth! We are expecting for Evrett to come home the week before Christmas, 285 days after he was readmitted to PICU at the beginning of March. My heavenly Father is amazing. His works are wondrous, unfathomable, and without number! I have seen the Lord heal my grandson in ways that simply have astonished the doctors, but the Lord is not finished. We were promised a seven part creative miracle. My grandson WILL have the third part of his brain. My grandson WILL walk. My grandson WILL talk. My grandson WILL ride a bicycle and play with his sisters! I serve a God who sent his Son, Jesus Christ, to take our infirmities, and bare our sicknesses, so we do not have to.

I cannot answer the questions as to why my grandson was not healed while he was still in his mother's womb or immediately after his birth. I cannot answer the questions as to why my grandson has been in the hospital so long or why his little body has endured so much sickness. I cannot answer the questions as to why my children have had to suffer through this sorrow or why our family has had to go through this broken-heartedness. I do not have any answers for those questions other than the answer Jesus gave us in John 10:10: the thief comes to steal, kill, and destroy. I do not focus, nor do I dwell on those questions. I set my heart on the promises of the Father and the comforting hope I have in my Savior, Jesus Christ. I am settled in the words of the Apostle Paul in 2 Timothy 1:12— For this reason, even though I suffer as I do, I am not ashamed; for I know in whom I have believed, and I am convinced that he is able to guard what I have entrusted to him until that day...*My God Reigns!*

Author's Note

Faith in the name of Jesus is the greatest gift we have been given. Faith in that name brings salvation, healing, restoration, and deliverance. Only through Jesus are we able to be comforted with a peace that passes understanding. Peace *is* possible in the midst of your most hopeless moments and darkest hours. Simply turn to Jesus, the good Shepherd.

I am a living witness to the goodness of Jesus Christ. My life was forever changed when I received the gift of salvation over 27 years ago. I am no different from many of you reading this book. I have encountered heartbreak and disappointment. I have been betrayed by those closest to me. I have been rejected, despised, and had all manner of evil said about me by family members, church members, and community members. BUT, my Lord has never left me, nor forsaken me. He has been with me every step of the way. He has turned my darkest moments into the greatest blessings of my life. He has turned my most difficult trials into the most beautiful treasures. My Lord has continually brought peace, comfort, and restoration to my life in times when it seemed as though the darkness, hurt, and destruction would never cease.

I can most assuredly declare without any doubt that I have the answer to your heartbreak. I have the answer to your sickness or disease. I have the answer to the healing or miracle you or your loved one needs. I have the answer to your loneliness and emptiness. I have the answer to your anger and unforgiveness. I have the answer to all your fears. I have the answer to your darkness, depression, and hopelessness. It is a never-fail answer. This answer works every time, for everyone, everywhere. The answer is Jesus!